öbv

Prime Time

Workbook 1

Georg Hellmayr
Elisabeth Scharf
Stephan Waba
Martina Zauner

www.oebv.at

Contents

1 My English words

Write the words in the correct boxes.

~~car park~~ acrobat city pilot film tablet hamburger cap tennis microphone chatting sneakers pizza mother hotel hockey doctor brother golf jeans computer sister orange juice game

Family	Free time	Food and drink	Electronics

Sports	Shopping	Jobs	Places
			car park

2 What I can do with English

Match the verbs on the left with the words on the right. Then write sentences. Start with *I can …*

1. watch		a crazy song.	I can	watch	an interesting video.
2. sing		a funny game.			
3. talk to		an English book.			
4. eat		a teacher.			
5. drink	1	an interesting video.			
6. read		an orange.			
7. play		a glass of water.			

This is me

3 My new friends

a) Complete the dialogue.

Max: Are you [1] Tarik?

Tarik: Yes, I am.

Max: ______ [2] Ingrid?

Lia: No, I'm not. I'm Lia.

Max: Tarik, how old ______ [3] ?

Tarik: ______ [4] ten years old.

Max: Where ______ [5] from?

Tarik: ______ [6] from Afghanistan.

Max: ______ [7] in class 1A?

Tarik: No, I'm not. ______ [8] in 1B.

Max: Lia, ______ [9] from Syria?

Lia: No, I'm not. ______ [10] from Iraq.

Max: ______ [11] in my class?

Lia: Yes, ______ [12] .

Tip

I'm = I **am**
you're = you **are**
he's = he **is**
she's = she **is**
they're = they **are**

b) Max talks about Tarik and Lia. Fill in:

She's (2x) • ~~is~~ • They're • 1B • is from (2x) • is • my • He's (2x)

This is [1] Tarik and this ______ [2] Lia. ______ [3] my new friends. Tarik ______ [4] Afghanistan. ______ [5] ten years old. ______ [6] in class ______ [7] . Lia ______ [8] Iraq. ______ [9] eleven years old. ______ [10] in ______ [11] class.

c) Read task 3b again and write a text about your friend(s) in your exercise book.

4 Countries and their flags

Write the missing letters.

1. G r e a t B r i t a i n
2. _ S _
3. _ t _ ly
4. C _ o a _ i _

In class

5 Classroom language

Write the phrases below the pictures.

1. Close the window.
2. ______________
3. ______________
4. ______________

6 The symbols in my English books

Match the sentences with the symbols.

1.	[ ]	I'm very good at this.
2.	[1]	Find online material for this task.
3.	[ ]	Find this listening online.
4.	[ ]	Work with a partner.
5.	[ ]	Work in a group with your partners.
6.	[ ]	This is a speaking task.

7 Focus on form: *a – an*

4.13 dx2c72

a) Listen carefully and repeat.

a	a sandwich	a doughnut	a unit in my book	a video	a green apple
an	an acrobat	an egg	an ice cream	an orange	an ugly monster

b) Now listen again and highlight the first letter of the words after *an*.

c) Let's practise. Fill in *a* or *an*.

1. a photo
2. an egg sandwich
3. ___ funny exercise
4. ___ elephant
5. ___ useful phrase
6. ___ old English song
7. ___ apple
8. ___ big orange
9. ___ animal
10. ___ red apple
11. ___ English book
12. ___ interesting story

4.14 vt6v5z

d) Listen and check.

Tip

u = [ju] → **a** a unit
u = [ʌ] → **an** an umbrella

To be

8 Focus on form: *am – is – are*

4.15 yh49f5

a) Listen and repeat in the gap.

b) Fill in *am*, *is*, *are* in the right gap.

1. I ___am___ from Great Britain.
2. Hi, Alma! Hi, Hamid! ______ you football fans? – Yes, we ______ .
3. Oh no! All my school things ______ on the floor.
4. Alma, Hamid and Connie ______ eleven years old.
5. Alma ______ in class 1C.
6. Rory ______ from New York.
7. Where ______ you from, Nessie?
8. I ______ from Scotland.
9. My schoolbag ______ cool.

9 Some personal pronouns

Fill in the words from the boxes in the right gaps.

he | ~~she~~ | it | we | they (2x)

1. Xenia is from the USA. ___She___ is very nice.
2. This is my new smartphone. ______ is so cool.
3. Celia and Toby are friends. ______ are in my class.
4. Robin is a basketball player. ______ is fantastic.
5. Babs and I are in the park now. ______ are playing football.
6. Please bring me my earphones, Boris. ______ are on the desk.

Check out

10 Vocabulary

Find the nine hidden words from unit 1 and circle them.
Look in these directions: ↓ →
Write them in your exercise book.

	A	B	C	D	E	F	G	H	I	J	K
1	M	Q	L	C	B	H	W	D	S	V	C
2	Z	T	N	F	I	T	L	A	G	E	I
3	R	B	V	X	K	P	C	R	F	Y	T
4	P	R	I	E	E	G	Z	W	K	N	Y
5	F	H	L	L	R	A	X	O	W	N	F
6	T	S	L	H	G	T	B	R	C	T	V
7	I	T	A	R	Y	O	Y	L	E	S	N
8	M	S	G	A	T	E	Q	D	R	Z	X
9	E	L	E	V	E	N	R	C	K	P	L
10	Y	T	F	T	E	E	N	A	G	E	R
11	F	Z	S	C	M	P	R	S	N	Q	V

☺ 😐 ☹ I can write new words correctly.
Ich kann neue Wörter richtig schreiben.

11 Me and my classmates

Mario Canelli brings two friends home. His dad opens the door to them. Decide who says what and put the dialogue in the correct order.

Mario	1	Hi Dad, this is Rudi.
______		What about you? What's your name?
______		Hi, Mr Canelli.
______		My name's Harry.
______		Thank you, Mr Canelli.
______		Harry? Nice name.
______		Hi, Rudi.
Mr Canelli	8	Right, off you go. Get yourselves some drinks.

☺ 😐 ☹ I can understand a dialogue about my friends.
Ich kann einen Dialog über meine Freunde verstehen.

☺ = I'm very good at this.
😐 = I can do this.
☹ = I need help.

My schoolbag

1 Don't forget!

a) Marcia needs many things for school. Look at the checklist. What has she got in her room? Tick ✓ the things on her list.

- [x] 1 schoolbag
- [ ] 1 pencil case
- [ ] 2 pens
- [ ] 1 blue and red eraser
- [ ] 3 green exercise books
- [ ] 1 glue stick
- [ ] 6 crayons
- [ ] 4 pencils
- [ ] 1 pair of scissors

b) Look at the picture. What does Marcia have to buy? Complete the shopping list.

one 1 pencil case 2

______ 3 blue and red eraser

______ 4 ______ 5 exercise books

______ 6 crayons

______ 7 pencils

2 Colours, colours, colours

a) Look at the snake and find the colours. Mark the words in the right colours.

b) Write the colours from above in your exercise book and draw school things in that colour.

My classroom

3 Marcel and Jezebel

Marcel and Jezebel need new lines for their rap. Can you help them?

open	close	clean	take out	put away	turn off
the door the window your books the cupboard		the board the window the desk the floor	your books your pencil cases your mobile phones your erasers your rulers		your mobile phones the computer the CD player

Marcel	Jezebel
Please, open 1 the door!	No, ______ 2 open the door!
Please, close the ______ 3 !	No, don't ______ 4 the window!
Please, ______ 5 the desk.	No, don't clean the ______ 6 .
Please, take out your ______ 7 phones!	No, don't ______ 8 out your mobile phones!
Please, put ______ 9 your rulers.	No, don't ______ 10 away your rulers.
Please, turn off the CD ______ 11 .	No, don't turn ______ 12 the CD player!

4 Mini dialogues

Match the questions with the answers. Write the numbers in the correct boxes.

1. What colour is your schoolbag, Joe?
2. Have you got a **green** pencil, Sue?
3. Where is my ruler, Mum?
4. Is your school building very big?
5. What colour is the board?
6. Where are my **blue** books?

- [ ] It's in your schoolbag.
- [ ] Yes, it is. It's got three floors.
- [1] My schoolbag is **yellow** and **black**.
- [ ] No, I'm sorry. I've only got a **pink** and a **blue** one.
- [ ] Look, there. Your books are on your desk.
- [ ] The board in our classroom is **green**.

My school

5 Hidden message

a) Find and circle the words from the green boxes. ↓↑ ↘↙ →←

BOARD CAFETERIA CARETAKER
CLASSROOM CRAYON ERASER
GLOBE GLUE LIBRARY
OFFICE RULER ~~SCHOOLBAG~~
TEACHER STUDENT

	A	B	C	D	E	F	G	H	I	J	K
1	C	C	R	U	L	E	R	G	T	T	M
2	H	A	A	E	R	E	L	A	N	O	O
3	R	E	F	R	M	U	I	I	E	F	O
4	C	E	I	E	E	N	B	T	D	F	R
5	H	E	S	C	T	T	R	H	U	I	S
6	D	R	A	O	B	E	A	O	T	C	S
7	T	E	A	C	H	E	R	K	S	E	A
8	C	R	A	Y	O	N	Y	I	E	O	L
9	L	E	B	O	L	G	C	A	A	R	C
10	S	C	H	O	O	L	B	A	G	F	E
11	T	E	R	R	E	S	A	R	E	I	A

b) Then use the leftover letters and complete the sentence below.

T H _ _ _   _ _ _   _ _ _ _   _ _   _ _ _

_ _ _ _ _ _   _ _ _ _ _ _ _ _ _

6 Where are all the things?

a) Complete the mind map: Where are these things?

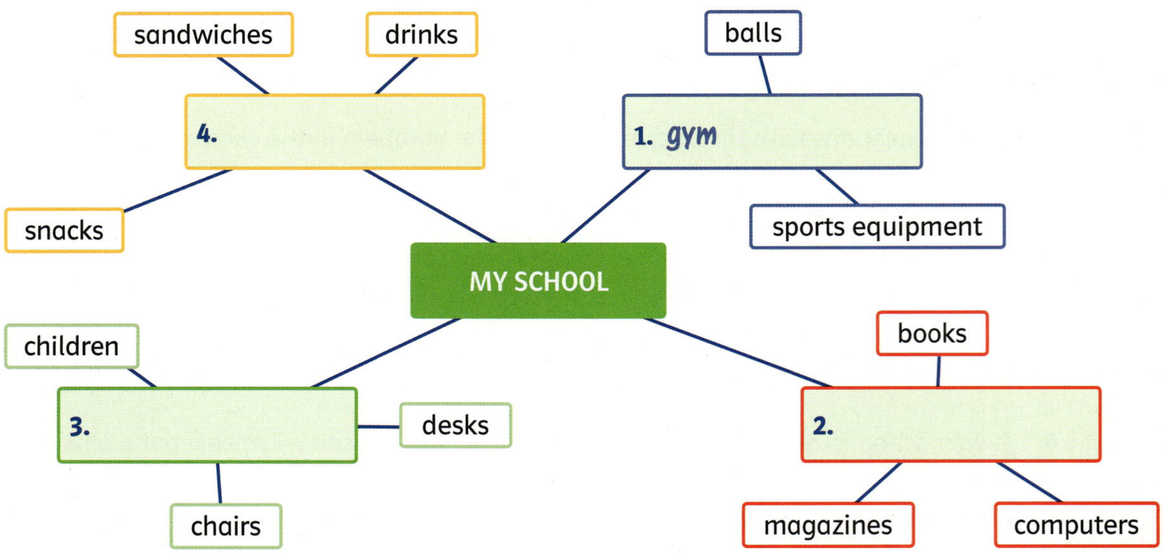

b) Then write questions and answers in your exercise book. Start like this:

Are there many desks and chairs in the classroom?
Yes, there are.

What I can do with English

7 Focus on form: *a* or *an*?

What is in Jason's schoolbag? Write the words in the correct boxes!

~~eraser~~ pencil box of crayons orange ruler pen English book
apple pencil case exercise book glue stick pair of scissors

a	an
	eraser

8 This is me!

a) Put the dialogues in the correct order.

Dialogue 1

- [ ] No, I'm in class 1a.
- [ ] My name's Mia!
- [ ] I'm ten years old too. Are you in class 1c?
- [ ] I'm from the Czech Republic.
- [ ] Where are you from, Mia?
- [ ] That's a nice name. How old are you?
- [1] Hello! What's your name?
- [ ] I'm ten years old.

Dialogue 2

- [ ] I'm from Switzerland. And what about you?
- [ ] My parents are from Serbia.
- [ ] Hi! What's your name?
- [ ] I'm ten years old. How old are you?
- [ ] I'm Boris. I'm in class 1D.
- [ ] I'm eleven. Where are you from?
- [ ] Really? Me too. How old are you?
- [ ] My name is Marco. What's your name?

b) Then copy one of the dialogues in your exercise book. Write the names of the speakers.

Working with words

9 School words

a) Study the mind map below. Draw pictures next to the words.

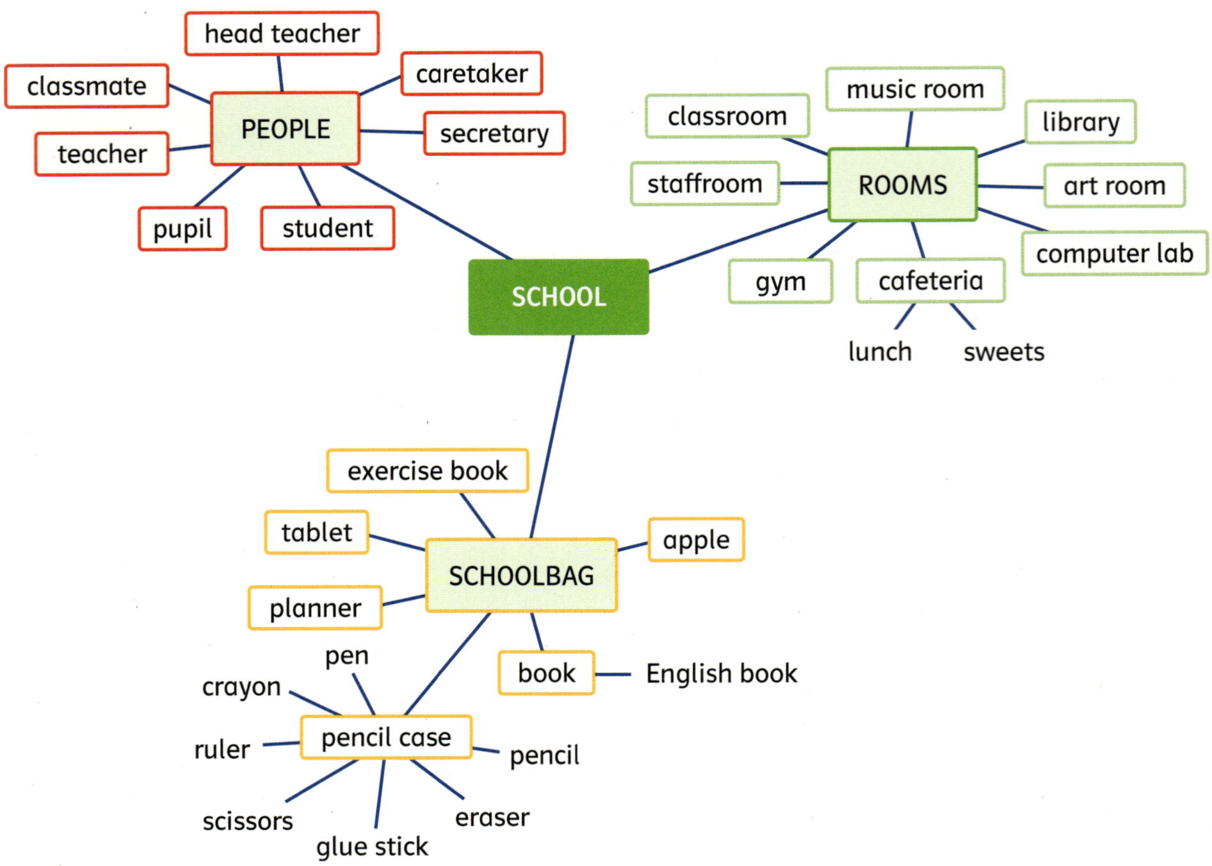

c) Make your own mind map below.

CLASSROOM

Check out

10 Listening: My school

4.16 y2nc2f

Krystal is describing her school. Listen and circle the correct answers.

1.	Krystal is	a) 10 years old.	b) 11 years old. (circled)	c) 12 years old.
2.	Her school is in	a) London.	b) Brighton.	c) Liverpool.
3.	She is in	a) year 6.	b) year 7.	c) year 8.
4.	Her classroom is on	a) the first floor.	b) the second floor.	c) the third floor.
5.	The computer lab is on	a) the first floor.	b) the second floor.	c) the third floor.
6.	The headteacher's office is on	a) the first floor.	b) the second floor.	c) the third floor.
7.	There is also a	a) library.	b) cafeteria.	c) film club.

☺ 😐 ☹ I can understand spoken texts about school.
Ich kann gesprochene Texte zum Thema Schule verstehen.

11 In my classroom

Write the correct sentences under the pictures.

There are two 1 green pencils on 2 the desk.

There is a ______ 3 ruler ______ 4 the bin.

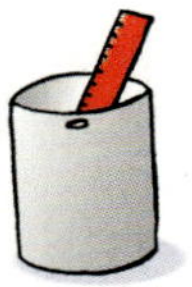

There are three books ______ 5 the bookshelf.

There is a crocodile ______ 7 the ______ 8.

There is a CD player ______ 6 the globe.

There is an ______ 9 ______ 10 my schoolbag.

☺ 😐 ☹ I can say where things are.
Ich kann ausdrücken, wo sich Dinge befinden.

☺ = I'm very good at this.
😐 = I can do this.
☹ = I need help.

The Happy Family Show

1 Robert's family

a) **Clare and Robert are talking about a family picture. Find the right questions for these answers.**

And who's the boy on your left? | Are they your father's parents? | How old is she? | Is this your granddad? | Who's that? | ~~Who's the girl on your right?~~

Clare: That's a nice picture. *Who's the girl on your right?* 1
Robert: Ah, this is my cousin Samantha. She is a great music lover.

Clare: ______________________ 2
Robert: Well, that is Ian, he is Samantha' s brother. He is a funny guy. He likes reading a lot. Their parents are Sue and Michael. Aunt Sue is my father's sister.

Clare: And the old lady behind you? ______________________ 3
Robert: This is my grandmother. We call her Granny Matilda.

Clare: ______________________ 4
Robert: She is 76. But she is still going strong.

Clare: And the old man next to her? ______________________ 5
Robert: Yes, that's right. He is 77. Funny, eh?

Clare: ______________________ 6
Robert: No, they aren't. They're my mother's parents, and they're also Samantha and Ian' s grandparents.
Clare: Nice family.

b) **Now Clare writes a text about Robert's family. But she makes some mistakes. Highlight the mistakes in Clare's text. Use the dialogue in task 1a to help you.**

Robert's family is not very big. He has no brothers or sisters, and he has only got one cousin. Her name is Samantha. Her parents are Sue and Michael. They are the children of Granny Matilda. Granny Matilda is 76 and her husband is 78. And there is Ian, Robert's brother. He likes reading. And there are his parents. Granny Matilda and her husband are his father's parents.

c) **Write Clare's text again and correct the mistakes.**

____

____

____

____

Family tree

2 Word search: Family members

a) Circle the twenty family members hidden in the grid. →← ↓↑

	A	B	C	D	E	F	G	H	I	J	K	L	M	N
1	G	R	A	N	D	P	A	D	A	D	E	M	R	R
2	N	O	S	D	N	A	R	G	E	F	I	W	E	E
3	M	H	Q	G	R	E	T	S	I	S	Y	Z	T	H
4	U	R	E	H	T	O	M	D	N	A	R	G	H	T
5	M	R	E	H	T	O	R	B	O	V	O	L	G	A
6	S	T	N	E	R	A	P	D	N	A	R	G	U	F
7	M	O	T	H	E	R	R	E	H	T	A	F	A	D
8	N	I	S	U	O	C	U	N	C	L	E	Q	D	N
9	V	H	H	D	N	A	B	S	U	H	N	O	S	A
10	R	E	T	H	G	U	A	D	D	N	A	R	G	R
11	A	M	D	N	A	R	G	B	Q	A	U	N	T	G

b) Write the words correctly. Each line stands for one letter.

1. b r o t h e r

2. u _ _ _ e

3. m _ _ _ _ _

4. c _ _ _ _ _

5. _ _ _ _ _ m _

6. h _ _ _ _ _ _

7. _ _ _ _ _ p _

8. d _ _ _ _ _ _ _

9. _ _ _ _ _ d _ _ _ _ _ _ _

10. _ _ n

11. m _ _

12. _ a _

13. _ _ s _ _ _

14. _ _ _ _ _ s _ _

15. _ _ _ _ _ m _ _ _ _ _

16. _ _ _ _ _ _ a _ _ _ _

17. _ _ _ _ _ p _ _ _ _ _ _

18. a _ _ _

19. w _ _ _

20. _ a _ _ _ _

CB p. 29

My best friend

3 The Fairfax family

a) **Read the story of the Fairfax family again and make a list of the people and animals at the party (→ coursebook p. 29).**

1. Mum
2. ______
3. ______
4. ______
5. ______
6. ______
7. ______
8. ______

b) **Now write one sentence about the people and animals.**

1. Zoe is Steve's sister.
2. Milly ______
3. Scottie ______
4. Lisa ______
5. Phil ______
6. Lisa and Phil ______
7. Steve ______
8. Mr Fairfax ______
9. Mrs Fairfax ______
10. Mr and Mrs Fairfax ______

4 Writing: My best friend

Use the sentences below and write a text about your best friend.

… is my best friend.
He / She is ten / eleven / twelve … years old.
He / She has got … brothers and sisters.
His / her dad / mum is … years old.
They live in … .
They have … pet/s.
He / She is great fun.
I like him / her a lot.

5 Focus on vocabulary: Interview

a) Complete the following text.

come from • school • ~~show~~ • sisters • father • How
I'm not • mother • speak • twins • question

Lawrence: Hi, welcome to our radio show "The big surprise". My name is Lawrence. Today we have an interesting surprise guest on our ___show___ 1. Good morning, Sandro.

Sandro: Hi, good morning.

Lawrence: Could you please tell us a little bit about yourself? Who are you? Where do you come from? ______ 2 old are you?

Sandro: Well, I'm thirteen years old, I ______ 3 California, and I go to ______ 4 in my local village. My name is Sandro because I'm from a Mexican-American family. My mother is Mexican, my ______ 5 is American.

Lawrence: Great, so you ______ 6 English and Spanish?

Sandro: Yes, I do. With my ______ 7 I speak Spanish, with my father I speak English, and when we're all together we speak Spanish or English.

Lawrence: Have you got any brothers and ______ 8 ?

Sandro: Yes, I have. I have two little sisters. They're ______ 9. They're seven years old.
(…)

Lawrence: Right, so let's find out what's so special about Sandro. Please call 089465283. *(…)* And here is the first caller. This is Diego from Pismo Beach. So what is your ______ 10 ?

Diego: Hi Sandro, are you a YouTube artist?

Sandro: No, ______ 11. Sorry. *(…)*

Lawrence: And here is the next caller …

4.17 8j4gj4

b) Now listen and check your answers.

6 Focus on form: Questions and answers

a) Underline the questions in the text above and answer them so that they are true about you.

b) Write your interview in your exercise book.

Check out

7 How old are the members of my family?

Read the text and fill the gaps with the right numbers. Write ✎ the words.

That's my mum (40).

That's my dad (34).

Clive (14), my older brother

That's me.

Ben (6), my little brother

Barro (3), our dog

Hi, my name is Leyla and I want to introduce my family to you. There are six of us, my mum, my dad, my ___two___ **1** brothers, me and our dog. My mother and my father are 74 years old together. My father is __________ **2** and my mother is __________ **3**. My little brother is __________ **4** and Clive, my older brother, is __________ **5**. The youngest member of our family is Barro, he is only __________ **6** years old.
To help us to get on the family show, send a text message to …

☺ 😐 ☹ I can use numbers and write them correctly.
Ich kann Zahlen verwenden und sie richtig schreiben.

8 Asking questions about families

Write ✎ questions for Benji's answers.

Claire: Hi, I'm Claire, ______________________________?
Benji: My name is Benji.

Claire: ______________________________?
Benji: I'm twelve years old.

Claire: ______________________________?
Benji: I come from Bosnia, and I go to school in Austria.

Claire: ______________________________?
Benji: Yes, I have a little brother and a baby sister.

☺ 😐 ☹ I can ask questions about personal details.
Ich kann Fragen zu einer Person stellen.

☺ = I'm very good at this.
😐 = I can do this.
☹ = I need help.

Time, time, time

1 Patricia's diary

Patricia has many things to do. Look at her diary and complete the dialogue.

	Monday	Tuesday	Wednesday	Thursday	Friday
09:00–12:00	school	school	school	school	school
12:00–15:00	13:15–14:00 piano lesson		12:45–14:15 Spanish course	12:30 lunch with Dad	12:30–13:30 shopping with Mum
15:00–18:00		17:30 cinema	18:00 dinner with Granny	17:15 volleyball class	

David: Hi Patricia! Do you want to go to the zoo with me next week?

Patricia: Yes, of course. Great idea!

David: Super! Can we go on Monday at half past one [1] (13:30)?

Patricia: I'm sorry, I can't. My piano lesson is from ______ [2] to ______ [3].

David: Okay, no problem. Are you free on Tuesday in the afternoon?

Patricia: On Tuesday I'm going to the cinema at ______ [4].

David: Hmm … I have school until ______ [5] (14:45) on Tuesday. How about Wednesday?

Patricia: Wednesday is not good. My Spanish course is from ______ [6] to ______ [7].

David: Can we go on Friday?

Patricia: Yes, okay. That's fine.

The things we usually do

2 Daily routines

Read the e-mails from Donald and his penfriend Betty and write the sentences below.

To: betty.b@littlemail.co.nz **Date:** 12 November | 19:03
Subject: My day

Hi Betty,

How are you? You want to know about my day, right? Well, I usually get up at 6 o'clock, even at the weekend, because I often do sports in the morning. Before I go to school, I always feed my cat "Duchess". She is four years old and sometimes sleeps in my bed. After school I often meet my friends in the park. We sometimes play basketball together. In the evening I usually have dinner with my family. We never eat meat because I'm a vegetarian.

How about you? Let me know.
Bye, Don

To: donald_myers@wlnet.at **Date:** 12 November | 21:42
Subject: RE: My day

Hi Don,

Great to hear from you. ☺ It's so cool that you have a cat. I don't have any pets. ☹
My day starts at seven o'clock. I never get up very early because my school is next door. I always walk to school. It just takes me two minutes. I often make breakfast for my younger brother and sister. After school I usually do my homework. Sometimes I hang out with friends, and we watch TV together. I never have dinner with all my family because my mum and my dad often work in the evening.

See ya!
xxx
----
sent from my smartphone

1. do homework after school: Betty usually does her homework after school.
2. do sports in the morning: ______________________.
3. get up very early: ______________________.
4. make breakfast: ______________________.
5. have dinner with the family: ______________________.
6. walk to school: ______________________.
7. eat meat: ______________________.
8. parents / work in the evening: ______________________.
9. feed the cat: ______________________.

Hooray – it's the weekend!

3 Weekends, weekends

a) Put the questions in the correct order and write them down.

1. weekend • When • the • does • start *When does the weekend start?*
2. come • together • When • the • boys • do

   ______________________________ ?
3. When • sleepover • is • time ______________________________ ?
4. do • When • we • late • sleep • always

   ______________________________ ?
5. When • make • we • do • the • plans • for • next • weekends

   ______________________________ ?

b) Check with the song "Weekends, weekends" (→ coursebook p. 36, task 9) and answer the questions in your exercise book.

The weekend starts on Friday at three.

4 Weekdays – weekends …

a) Freddy and Tina have a lot to do at the weekend – but also on weekdays. Write questions and answers to the pictures.

Monday, 16.15

Wednesday, 12.30

Thursday, 15.00

When do Freddy and Tina often *listen to music* 1 ? On Monday at *quarter past four* 2 .

When ________ 3 always ________ 4 ? On ________ 5 .

________ 6 sometimes ________ 7 ? ________ 8 .

b) Write down what they do on Monday, Wednesday and Thursday in your exercise book.

Where is ...? Where are ...?

5 Focus on form: Miruna's mess

a) Ask questions: Where are Miruna's things?

b) Answer the questions.

1. CD player: *Where is Miruna's CD player?* *It's under the bed.* (bed)
2. packet of tomato juice: ______________________________?
   ______________________________. (bookshelf)
3. football: ______________________________?
   ______________________________. (bin)
4. vampire book: ______________________________?
   ______________________________. (alarm clock)
5. toothbrush: ______________________________?
   ______________________________. (desk)
6. black dress: ______________________________?
   ______________________________. (schoolbag)
7. sandwich: ______________________________?
   ______________________________. (desk)

Working with words

PAST	TO

6 Times of the day

Word bank

a.m. = 0.00 – 12.00 (in the) morning
p.m. = 12.00 – 0.00 (in the) afternoon, (in the) evening
(at) night

a second • a minute • an hour • a day • a week • a month • a year

a) Put the following times in the correct order.

- [ ] ten past three
- [1] three o'clock
- [ ] a quarter past three
- [ ] half past three
- [ ] a quarter to four
- [ ] twenty to four
- [ ] four o'clock

b) Write the words under the correct headings.

~~at eight o'clock in the morning~~ · before going to bed · at night · before school starts · after school · in the afternoon · before lunchtime · from three to four in the afternoon

a.m.	p.m.
at eight o'clock in the morning	

Check out

7 Listening: My day

4.18 bf89np

Joyce talks about her day. Listen and circle the correct answers.

1. Joyce wakes up at	**a)** 6.30.	**b)** 6.15.	**c)** 6.45.
2. At a quarter to seven she	**a)** listens to music.	**b)** brushes her teeth.	**c)** goes to school.
3. She has breakfast at	**a)** 7.00.	**b)** 7.30.	**c)** 7.15.
4. She goes to school	**a)** with her dad.	**b)** by bus.	**c)** by bike.
5. School starts at	**a)** 8.45.	**b)** 8.30.	**c)** 9.00.
6. Her favourite lunch is	**a)** a salad.	**b)** a sandwich.	**c)** pasta.
7. When she comes home, she	**a)** reads a book.	**b)** plays games.	**c)** plays the piano.
8. She goes to bed at	**a)** 8.30.	**b)** 9.30.	**c)** 9.00.

I can understand texts about daily routines.
Ich kann Texte über tägliche Gewohnheiten verstehen.

8 Asking questions

Ask and answer questions about Howard's day.

1. *When does Howard get up?*

At half past six.

2. ______________________________?

______________________________.

3. ______________________________?

______________________________.

4. ______________________________?

______________________________.

I can ask and answer questions about daily routines.
Ich kann zu täglichen Gewohnheiten Fragen stellen und beantworten.

☺ = I'm very good at this.
😐 = I can do this.
☹ = I need help.

In a corner shop

1 Listening: Can I help you?

a) Fill in the gaps.

a pound of • anything • change • else • ~~help you~~ • here • muffins • sorry • take • thanks • that's

Shop assistant: Hello. Can I ___help you___ 1 ?

Customer: Yes, ______________ 2 strawberries, please.

Shop assistant: Here you are. ______________ 3 else?

Customer: Yes, two ______________ 4 , please.

Shop assistant: ______________ 5 , we don't have any muffins today.

Customer: Okay. Then I'll ______________ 6 a doughnut.

Shop assistant: A doughnut. Anything ______________ 7 ?

Customer: No, ______________ 8 .

Shop assistant: ______________ 9 three pounds forty.

Customer: ______________ 10 you are, thanks.

Shop assistant: And here's your ______________ 11 . Thanks very much.

4.19 3ev9dr **b) Listen to the dialogue and check your answers.**

2 How much is …? How much are …?

Write down five dialogues in your exercise book.

In a supermarket

3 Packs and pounds

Write the words in the right boxes.

~~bananas~~ baked beans blackberries cheese crisps cherries doughnuts lemonade lollies milk muffins orange juice oranges strawberries sweets tomato juice tomato soup

packet of	bottle of	kilo of / pound of	tin of
		bananas	

4 Shopping dialogues

a) Put the dialogues in the right order.

b) Write them in your exercise book.

Dialogue 1

- [ ] Thanks very much. Do you know how much they are?
- [ ] Thanks!
- [ ] You can find them in the fruit and vegetable section.
- [ ] Yes, they're £1.99 a pound
- [1] Excuse me, where can I get cherries?
- [ ] You're welcome.

Dialogue 2

- [ ] Sorry, I don't know.
- [ ] No problem. Thank you!
- [1] Excuse me, can you tell me where I can find some apple juice?
- [ ] Thanks a lot. Do you also have orange juice?
- [ ] You're welcome.
- [ ] Yes, of course. You can find it in the drinks section.

A farewell party for Clara

Yes, it does. | Yes, she does. | Yes, they do. | No, he doesn't. | No, she doesn't. | We don't know.

5 Questions and answers

Put the words in the correct order and write questions. Then answer the questions with the phrases on the right.

1. Sarah • does • buy • want • to • for • Clara's • party • a • top

   Does Sarah want to buy a top for Clara's party? Yes, she does.

2. like • does • Sarah • the • T-shirt • silver • print • with • the

   ______________________________?

   ______________________.

3. does • have • Sarah • enough • to • buy • the • T-shirt • money

   ______________________________?

   ______________________.

4. the • colour • does • like • Clara • yellow

   ______________________________?

   ______________________.

5. a • lot • of • does • with • zebra • stripes • the • T-shirt • money • cost

   ______________________________?

   ______________________.

6. does • pocket • money • Clara • all • her • spend

   ______________________________?

   ______________________.

7. Tony • give • Clara • a • box • of • does • chocolates

   ______________________________?

   ______________________.

8. and • Sarah • Clara • do • T-shirts • the • same • wear

   ______________________________?

   ______________________.

This is my chocolate

6 Focus on form: What we've got

a) Write sentences: What do they say? What can we see?

1. The clown says: "This is my chocolate, this is my balloon and this is my lolly ______."

   We can see: This is his chocolate, this is his balloon and this is his lolly ______.

2. The runners say: "This is our orange, ______."

   We can see: This is their orange, ______.

3. Granny says: "______."

   We can see: ______.

4. The girls say: "______."

   We can see: ______.

b) Ask questions and answer them.

	question	answer
1. clown, sweets	Has the clown got any sweets?	No, he hasn't.
2. runners, banana		
3. granny, doughnut		
4. girls, DVD		

Working with words

7 A bottle of milk, a packet of butter

a) Write the words under the pictures.

apples | bananas | biscuits | butter | chocolate | crisps | eggs | juice
~~milk~~ | nuts | oranges | sugar | tea | tomatoes | water

a bag of

______ ______ ______

a bottle of

milk ______ ______

a bar of

______

a box of

______

a can of
a tin of

______

a carton of

______ ______

a kilogram of / a pound of

______ ______

a packet of

______ ______ ______ ______

b) Copy the words in the correct boxes.

a bottle of	a packet of	a carton of	a kilogram of a pound of	a bag of
milk				

Check out

8 In a corner shop

Fill in the missing words.

Shop assistant: Hello there. Can I *help* 1 you?

Customer: A ________ 2 of milk, please.

Shop assistant: Here you are. Anything ________ 3 ?

Customer: Yes, two ________ 4 of strawberries, please.

Shop assistant: ________ 5 , we don't have any strawberries today.

Customer: Okay. Can I have two ________ 6 of chocolate then?

Shop assistant: Two bars of chocolate. ________ 7 else?

Customer: No, ________ 8 .

Shop assistant: ________ 9 two pounds twenty.

Customer: ________ 10 you are, thanks.

Shop assistant: And here's your ________ 11 . Thanks very much.

☺ 😐 ☹ I can take part in shopping dialogues.
Ich kann an Einkaufsdialogen teilnehmen.

9 Asking for the price

Here are the sentences from four dialogues. Write the dialogues in your exercise book.

~~How much are the cherries?~~ | ~~Thanks very much.~~ | ~~They are £2.99 a pound.~~

How much is a ruler? | Thanks very much. | How much is the cheese?

Thanks very much. | How much are the batteries? | It's fifty pence.

Thanks very much. | They are 99 pence each. | It's £1.89 a pound.

How much are the cherries? – They are £2.99 a pound. – Thanks very much.

☺ 😐 ☹ I can understand shopping dialogues.
Ich kann Einkaufsdialoge verstehen.

☺ = I'm very good at this.
😐 = I can do this.
☹ = I need help.

My games

1 Snakes and ladders

Info

Rules of the game

Ladders: Move forward to the other end of the ladder.
Snakes: Move back to the tail of the snake.
Question mark: Answer the questions on the activity cards.

a) Write activity cards. Copy the sentences in the green boxes on little cards.

Count from 1 to 10.

Ask for the price of a T-shirt.

Name five things in your school bag.

Count from 11 to 20.

Tell the time.

Name three rooms in a school.

Name three colours on the gameboard.

Name the days of the week.

b) Play the game with one or more partners.

1. Roll the dice to see who goes first. The highest score starts.
2. When you get to a box with a question mark (**?**), your partner picks an activity card and reads it out. If your answer is correct, you move to the next square. Check the answers with the book.
3. The winner is the first player to get to the FINISH.

Tip

What you need to play the game:
- two dice
- a game piece for each player

Quiz games

2 Questions and answers

a) Match the questions with the answers.

1.	How old are you?		He is sixty-six.
2.	How much is the pullover?		He gets up at half past six every day.
3.	What do they have for breakfast?		Yes, I do. Especially vampire stories.
4.	Where do you live?		It's twenty-three pounds.
5.	Does he have a pet?	1	I am eleven and my sister is three.
6.	When does your dad get up in the morning?		Roseanne loves cereals and Ben often has baked beans on toast.
7.	How old is your granddad?		No, she isn't.
8.	Do you like books?		Yes, he does. He's in a team.
9.	Does your brother play basketball?		I live in Styria.
10.	Is Silvia your best friend?		No, he doesn't.

b) How do you ask for the following information?

1. name: What's your name?

2. age: How ____________________ ?

3. address: ____________________ ?

4. pets: ____________________ ?

5. breakfast: ____________________ ?

6. sports: ____________________ ?

7. school: ____________________ ?

8. get up: ____________________ ?

Mime the action

3 What are the children doing?

a) Ask questions and write them down.

cooking | having a shower | listening to music | playing on your mobile | ~~sleeping~~ | talking on the phone

Rupert

Almira

Mona

Rupert, are you sleeping?

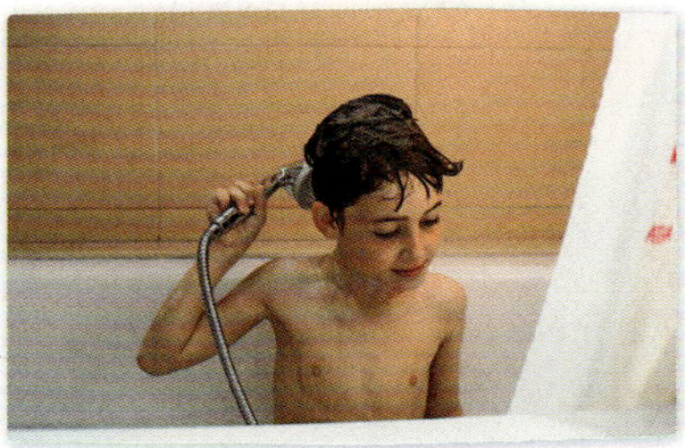

Steve

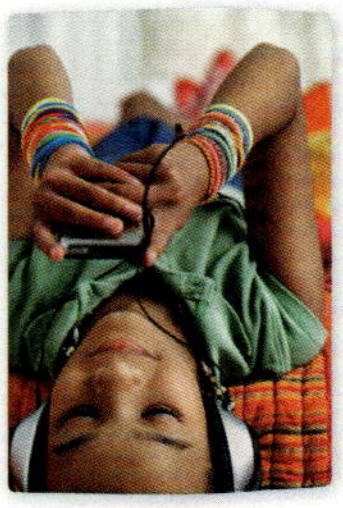

Julia

Silvana

4.20 8nz4g5

b) Listen and check.

c) Answer the questions below.

1. Is Rupert learning English? No, he isn't. He is sleeping.
2. Is Almira talking on the phone?
3. Is Mona riding her bike?
4. Is Steve reading a book?
5. Is Julia listening to music?
6. Is Silvana playing volleyball?

Fun times

4 Focus on form: Expressing time

a) **Ricarda goes to a special school where they play games all day long. Look at her timetable and complete the dialogue.**

	Monday	Tuesday	Wednesday	Thursday	Friday
8.45–10.00	CARD GAMES	MEMORY	BOARD GAMES	SNAKES AND LADDERS	COMPUTER GAMES
10.15–11.30	CHESS	COMPUTER GAMES	DRAUGHTS	NOUGHTS AND CROSSES	CROSSWORD PUZZLES
11.30–12.30	lunch	lunch	lunch	lunch	lunch
12.30–13.45	QUIZ GAMES	NOUGHTS AND CROSSES	CARD GAMES	BOARD GAMES	MEMORY
14.00–15.15	CROSSWORD PUZZLES	DOMINOES	QUIZ GAMES	LUDO	DOMINOES
15.30–16.45	SNAKES AND LADDERS	HAPPY FAMILIES	CHESS	CHESS	HAPPY FAMILIES

Ricarda: Hiya!
Boris: Hi Ricarda! How is your new school?
Ricarda: I love it there. There's no English, there's no maths. We have to play games all day long!
Boris: You play games all day long? You're kidding! Let's see … What do you do on Monday in period 2?

Ricarda: That's from *a quarter past ten* 1 to ______ ______ ______ 2. We play chess then. Chess makes you intelligent! We play it three times a week.
Boris: Do you also do crossword puzzles in school?

Ricarda: Of course. We do crossword puzzles every ______ 3 in the afternoon and every Friday in the ______ 4.
Boris: Is that your favourite subject?
Ricarda: No, I hate doing crossword puzzles! My favourite subject is playing draughts. It's every Wednesday before lunch, from ______ ______ ______ ______ 5 to ______ ______ ______ 6.
Boris: Wow. You must be really clever! Do you also play games during your lunch break?

Ricarda: No, we don't. From ______ ______ ______ 7 to ______ ______ ______ 8 we need a break from all these games!

b) **What is your favourite day at game school? Write about it in your exercise book! Write four sentences.**

My favourite day is Thursday. We play Snakes and Ladders from a quarter to nine to ….

Check out

5 Listening: My favourite game

4.21 c9tp8t

a) **Listen to Bob. He talks about his favourite game.**

b) **Read the sentences and circle the correct words and phrases.**

1. Bob's favourite game is **Scrabble** • **Monopoly**.
2. For this game you need game pieces, **sticks** • **dice** and of course the board.
3. There are also small plastic **houses** • **cars** and plastic hotels.
4. If you get to a square with a piece of **land** • **chocolate**, you can buy it.
5. If another player enters your piece of land, he or she **can** • **must** pay you money.
6. They often play it **in the holidays** • **at the weekend**.
7. They usually start on Saturday after **lunch** • **breakfast** and play until they have to go bed.
8. They continue on Sunday **at lunchtime** • **after breakfast**.
9. They often play until **three o'clock** • **the evening**.
10. Bob and his family love Monopoly because every game is **difficult** • **different**.

☺ 😐 ☹ I can understand texts about people's free time activities.
Ich kann Texte zu Freizeitaktivitäten von Menschen verstehen.

6 Reading: Game instructions

Number the instructions in the right order.

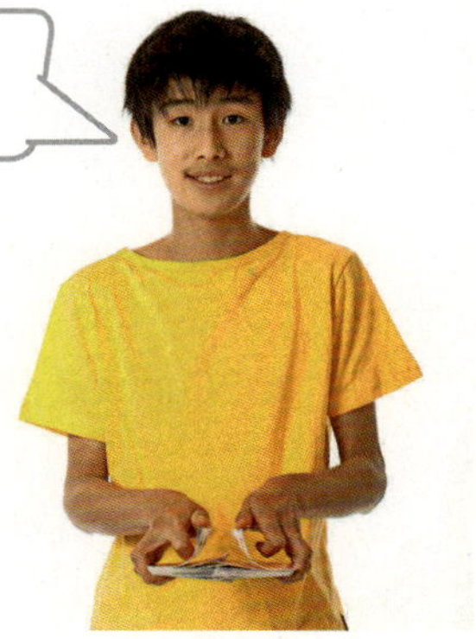

- [ ] The winner is the first player with no cards in his/her hands.
- [ ] First, shuffle the cards.
- [ ] If the answer is yes, the first player gets the card and can continue. If the answer is no, it's the other player's turn.
- [1] "Happy families" is a game for four players. There are 44 picture cards, and the players try to get sets of four cards.
- [ ] If a player has a complete set of four cards, he/she puts them on the table.
- [ ] Now the game can start: The first player asks another player for a card he/she needs.
- [ ] After that, every player gets 11 cards.

☺ 😐 ☹ I can understand game instructions.
Ich kann Spielanleitungen verstehen.

☺ = I'm very good at this.
😐 = I can do this.
☹ = I need help.

Unit 7 My time – my activities

Join the circus camp!

1 What we can/can't do

a) Match the sentence halves and then match the pictures.

1. I can do	☐	an instrument.
2. Amelie can juggle	☐	a horse.
3. My best friend can ride	☐	on a trapeze.
4. Amelie can't walk on	☐	with four balls.
5. Amelie can play	1	cartwheels.
6. My brother can't swing	☐	her hands.

A

B

C

1

D

E

F

b) Answer the questions with *Yes, I can.* or *No, I can't.*

1. Can you play an instrument? ______________________
2. Can you walk on a tightrope? ______________________
3. Can you do a cartwheel? ______________________
4. Can you swing on a trapeze? ______________________
5. Can you do a magic trick? ______________________

c) Use the activities in the green boxes and write about the things you can and can't do. Write two positive ☺ and two negative ☹ sentences in your exercise book.

do a handstand | play an instrument | ride a horse | walk on a tightrope | do a magic trick | juggle with three balls | swing on a trapeze | do cartwheels | walk on my hands

At the circus camp

2 What you are good at

a) Read the dialogues and put them in the correct order.

Dialogue 1:

- [ ] Yes, I am. What about you?
- [ ] That sounds cool. When is it?
- [ ] It's next Friday from 3 p.m. to 6 p.m.
- [1] Hello Maya. Are you good at juggling?
- [ ] Yes, I'm also good at juggling. That's why I'm interested in this circus workshop at school.
- [ ] Alright, let's go there together. I think it's great fun.

Dialogue 2:

- [ ] Wow! I'm not good at that, but I can play the flute.
- [ ] Sounds great. So let's sign up for the talent show. When is it?
- [ ] It's next Monday and it starts at 6 in the evening.
- [ ] I'm not good at playing an instrument, but I'm good at doing cartwheels.
- [1] Hey Joseph, there is a school talent show. Are you good at playing an instrument?
- [ ] Okay, so let's meet at five.

b) Look at the pictures and then complete the text below. Use one word for each gap.

These are my friends Antonio, Sena and Mike, and my name is Miranda. We all have got special talents. I'm really ___good___ 1 at playing instruments. My favourite instrument is the violin, but I also love ______ 2 the piano. My friend Antonio is good ______ 3 juggling because he can juggle with five balls at the same time. My best friend Sena is very good at ______ 4 cartwheels and swinging on a ______ 5. She loves doing sports. And there's Mike – he is really good ______ 6 doing magic tricks. He loves ______ 7 card tricks.

Miranda

Antonio

c) Look at the pictures and write sentences in your exercise book. Write one sentence for each of the children. Start like this:

Miranda is good at playing instruments. Antonio … .

Mike

Sena

The big performance

3 Be a circus star

a) Look at the word snake and find the words from "A magic trick" (→ coursebook p. 60).

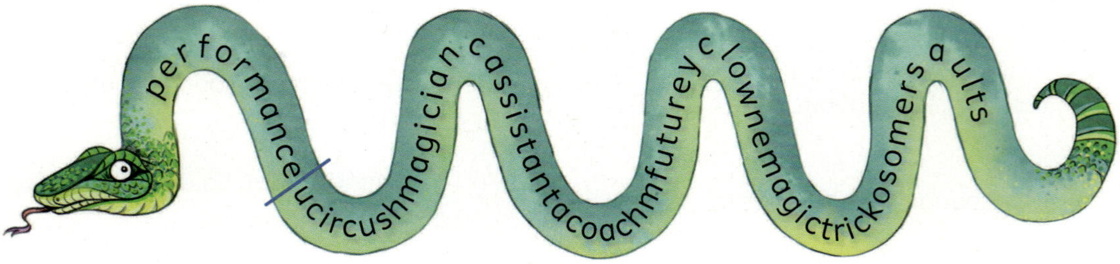

b) Go back to your coursebook p. 60 and read the story "A magic trick" again. Find the words and phrases in task 3a and highlight them in the text in your coursebook.

c) Complete the phrases below with the words from the text of "A magic trick".

1. watch the performance
2. good ________ ________ somersaults
3. good ________ ________ a clown
4. good ________ ________ magic tricks

d) Use the words from task 3a and fill in the gaps. Then put the sentences in the correct order.

[ ] Amelie is the magician **1** and Noah is her ________ **2**.

[ ] The clowns are very good at doing ________ **3** and juggling.

[ ] The ________ **4** stands in the middle of the tent and welcomes the people.

[ ] The people come into the big tent to watch the ________ **5**.

[1] The kids are nervous because tonight they must do a ________ **6**.

[ ] The coach says, "Hello. First, we have the ________ **7**!" The people clap.

[ ] Now it's the kids' turn. There's a big box in the middle of the ________ **8** ring.

[ ] In the ________ **9** the kids may be clowns, not magicians.

[ ] Amelie's trick doesn't work at all, but the people think it is funny, and they all laugh.

Likes and dislikes

4 Focus on form: What we love doing

Use the words in brackets and fill in the right plural forms.

1. Jimmy is my best friend. He loves travelling and visiting cities (city) all over the world.
2. Max and Jo love shopping. They always go shopping on ______ (Friday).
3. A lot of girls and ______ (boy) like playing games with their friends.
4. Tim and Karam have to buy a lot of ______ (battery) for their cameras.
5. Hannah loves cooking with ______ (cherry) and ______ (berry).

5 Focus on form: Do you like ...? – Does he/she like ...?

a) Read the dialogue and complete the gaps with *do* or *does*.

Bob: Hello Natalie, what's up?

Natalie: Hey Bob, do 1 you like playing ball games?

Bob: Yes, I ______ 2. Why?

Natalie: There is a sports camp on Saturday afternoon. We play ball games. ______ 3 you like playing volleyball and handball?

Bob: Yes, I ______ 4. Well, I'm really good at basketball and handball, but I hate playing volleyball.

Natalie: What about your sister? ______ 5 she like playing volleyball?

Bob: Yes, she really ______ 6. ______ 7 you want her to come, too?

Natalie: Yes, I ______ 8. That's a great idea. The camp starts at 3 p.m.

b) Read the dialogue again and answer the questions.

1. Does Bob like playing ball games? Yes, he does.
2. Do the children play basketball and football at the sports camp? ______ .
3. Does Bob like playing volleyball? ______ .
4. Does Bob hate playing handball? ______ .
5. Does Bob's sister like playing volleyball? ______ .

Working with words

6 My free time activities

Complete this table with at least four phrases from the mind map below.

I already know these phrases.	I would like to remember these phrases.

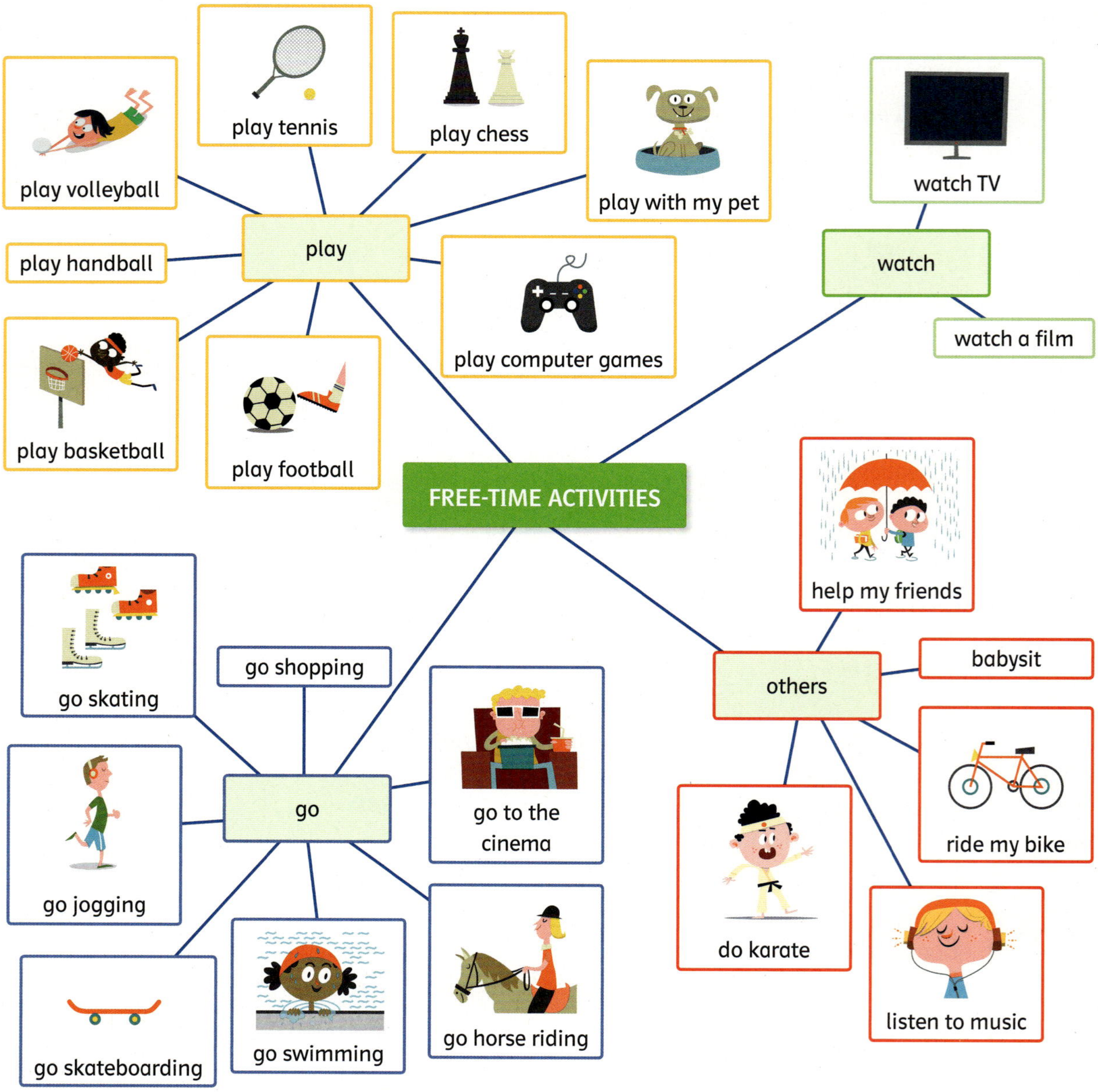

Check out

7 Language in use: What do the children like doing?

Match the sentence halves.

1. Marty likes reading	☐	to rock music, and she's good at playing the drums.
2. George loves drawing	☐	photographs of his pets.
3. Dan and Hamid like playing	☐	manga cartoons. He is very good at it.
4. Charlize loves listening	☐	their horses Chipsy and Caesar.
5. Meral and Chris love riding	☐	football. They're quite good at doing ball tricks.
6. My best friend likes taking	1	books. He's also good at reading fast.

☺ 😐 ☹ I can understand sentences about free time activities.
Ich kann Sätze zum Thema Freizeitaktivitäten verstehen.

8 Reading: What do children and teenagers like doing?

Read the text and then tick ✓ T (= true) or F (= false).

There are lots of different free time activities for teenagers and children. A lot of teenagers like hanging out with their friends. They like listening to music together or maybe playing computer games. A lot of children like shopping very much. Many children love reading; some like reading e-books and others like reading paper books. The book "Wimpy Kid", for example, is very famous, and lots of children love it. After school many children like playing games with their friends; for example ball games like football or basketball. They often play ball games at the park or in sports clubs. A lot of children also like playing instruments. Some are good at playing the piano or the guitar, others like singing and dancing.

	T (true)	F (false)
1. There are a lot of different activities that children do in their free time.	✓	☐
2. Children don't like hanging out with their friends.	☐	☐
3. Teenagers and children only read e-books and digital books.	☐	☐
4. After school many children like playing ball games with their friends.	☐	☐
5. Not many children like playing instruments.	☐	☐

☺ 😐 ☹ I can read and understand texts about free time activities.
Ich kann Texte über Freizeitaktivitäten lesen und verstehen.

☺ = I'm very good at this.
😐 = I can do this.
☹ = I need help.

At the doctor's

1 Parts of the body

Look at the pictures and do the crossword. Can you find the solution?

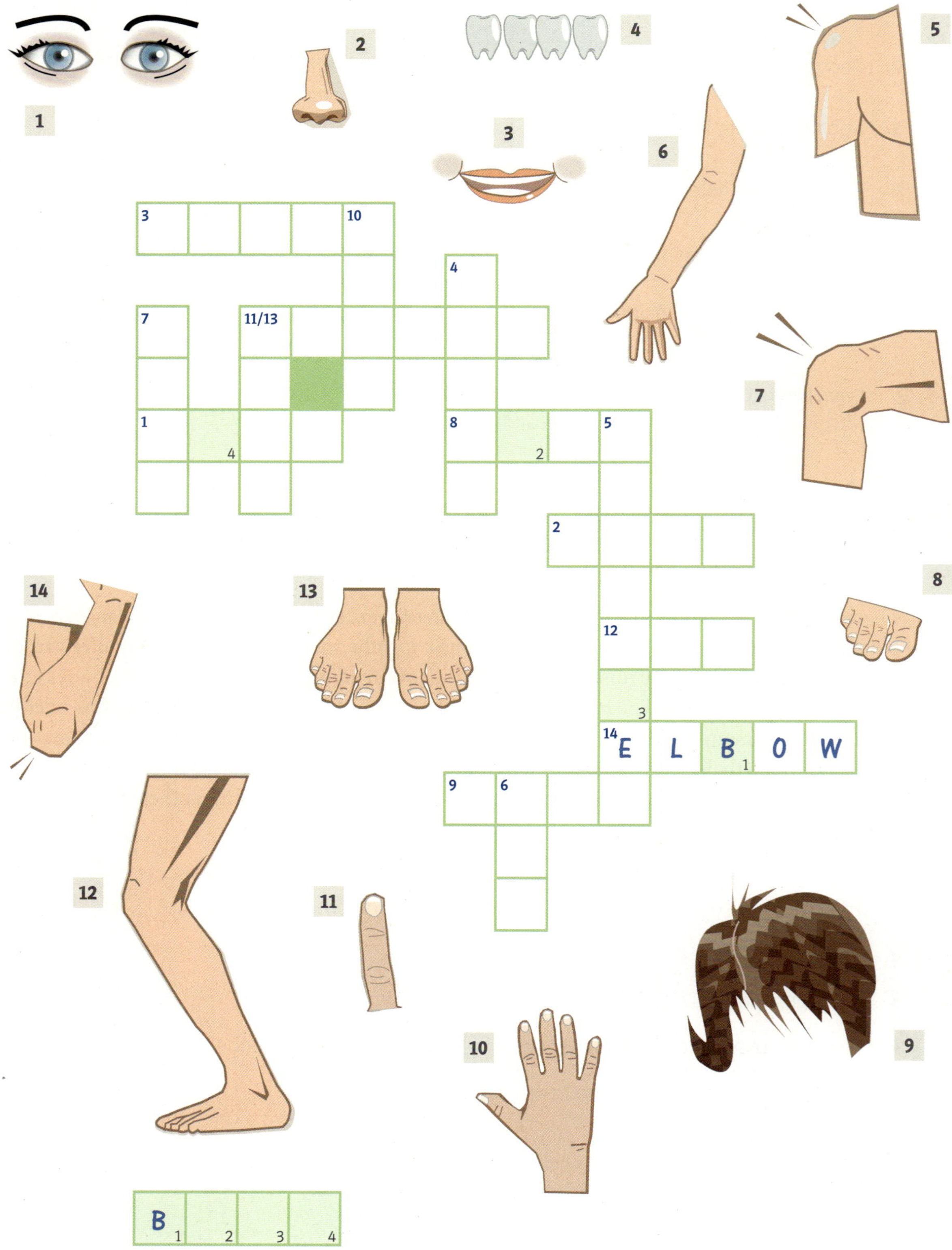

2 Illnesses

a) Look at the word snake and find the illnesses. Circle the words.

b) Use the words from task 2a and match them with the children. Write the illnesses.

1

Leo

____

2

Harriet

____

3

Loretta and Marietta

____

4

Trish

____

5

Oliver and Pete

____

6

Peter

sore throat

c) Complete the text about the children with the information from task 2b.

Poor Leo! He has got earache 1. Leo's best friend is Harriet, and she's sick, too. She has got ______ ______ ______ 2. Loretta and Marietta have got a problem with their teeth. They have got ______ 3. Trish doesn't feel well because her head hurts. She has got ______ ______ 4. Oliver and Pete are always hungry, and they eat a lot of food for dinner. Now they've got ______ ______ ______ 5. Peter can't go to school today because his throat hurts. He has got ______ ______ ______ 6.

CB p. 69

Look after your body

3 Being on a sports team

a) **Read the story "On the team" (→ coursebook p. 69) again and complete the words below.**

1. fo o t b a l ler
2. _ o _ ters
3. he _ d _ c _ e
4. t _ a _ p _ a _ er
5. m _ t _ h
6. te _ m _ or _

b) **Now find the words from task 3a in the text "On the team" and underline them.**

c) **Decide if the statements are true (T) or false (F).**

		T (true)	F (false)
1.	Sam Tucker wants to become a famous footballer.	✓	☐
2.	His football coach tells Sam to practise hard.	☐	☐
3.	Sam and his mother play football in the garden every day.	☐	☐
4.	Sam stays up late, watches lots of video clips and doesn't eat healthy food.	☐	☐
5.	His mum takes him to the doctor's because he has got stomach ache.	☐	☐
6.	The doctor tells Sam to eat healthy food and to get more sleep.	☐	☐
7.	When Sam is on the team, they win the first match of the season.	☐	☐
8.	Sam is good at teamwork and playing on a team.	☐	☐

d) **Correct the false sentences and write them in your exercise book.**

4 Keeping fit – what you should and shouldn't do

a) **Match the sentence halves.**

1.	You shouldn't stay	☐	vegetables and fruit every day.
2.	You should eat	☐	a lot of water.
3.	You shouldn't drink	☐	breakfast every morning.
4.	You should have	1	on the sofa all day long.
5.	You should drink	☐	videos and TV for more than two hours a day.
6.	You shouldn't watch	☐	a lot of sugary drinks like lemonade.

b) **What are your tricks to keep fit? Write four more tips in your exercise book.**

Talking about your body and health

5 Focus on form: What's wrong with you?

Read the mini dialogues below and complete them.

1. Dave: This is my brother. He always eats candy and now he doesn't feel well. He has **1** got stomach ache.

Doctor: Oh, really. Then he should drink peppermint tea and eat more fruit and vegetables, not sweets.

2. Maya: I've got a problem. There ________ **2** something wrong with my throat, it hurts so much.

Doctor: Ah, you ________ **3** got a sore throat. Then you should drink a lot of tea with honey!

3. Mum: These ________ **4** my sons Joe and Paul. They both feel very hot.

Doctor: Let me have a look. Well, they both ________ **5** a high temperature. They should stay in bed and rest.

4. Dad: This ________ **6** my daughter Louise. She ________ **7** got very bad earache. I think she is sick.

Doctor: Hmm. Let me see. Yes, she ________ **8**. Louise, I think you should stay in bed for three days.

6 Focus on form: Moodley, the monster

a) Read the story below and fill in the gaps with *and*, *but* or *because*.

This is my monster. His name is Moodley and **1** he lives alone. Moodley is a very nice monster, ________ **2** he hasn't got any friends. His favourite free time activity is eating noodles ________ **3** noodles are his favourite food. His head is yellow. He only has got one red eye, ________ **4** he has got four pink ears. His mouth is very small, ________ **5** his nose is really big. Moodley has got two green arms ________ **6** he has got two blue legs. His arms are very long, ________ **7** his legs are very, very short. He has got twelve fingers on each hand ________ **8** fifteen toes on each foot.

b) Draw your monster. Then write a text in your exercise book and answer the questions below. Start like this: *My monster's name is …*

1. What's your monster's name?
2. What's your monster's favourite food?
3. What colour is your monster's hair?
4. What colour are his/her arms and legs?
5. How many fingers/toes does your monster have?
6. What about mouth, lips, eyes and ears?

Working with words

7 What do you do with new words and phrases?

a) There are many ways to study vocabulary. Here are some tips and tricks how to practise and remember new English words.

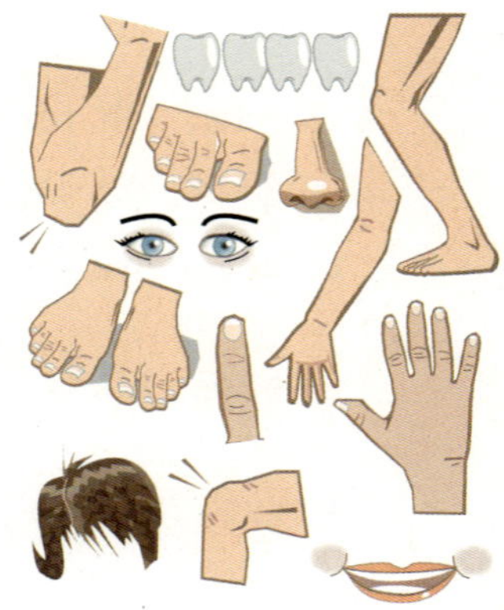

1. : Draw your own pictures of the words you want to remember and write the words in English. Put up the **drawings** in your room so you see them every day.
2. : If you aren't good at drawing, you can also cut out **pictures** from newspapers or magazines. You can also find nice pictures on the internet and print them out. Use pictures to work with new words and phrases.
3. + : Use your **hands** and your **voice**; for example: point at the body part and say the word.
4. + : Never forget that **practice makes perfect**. Try to practise as often as possible, but not for too long. It really helps if you practise new words/phrases for 10 to 15 minutes every day.

b) Use the grid below and draw five more words/phrases from unit 8 you want to practise and remember.

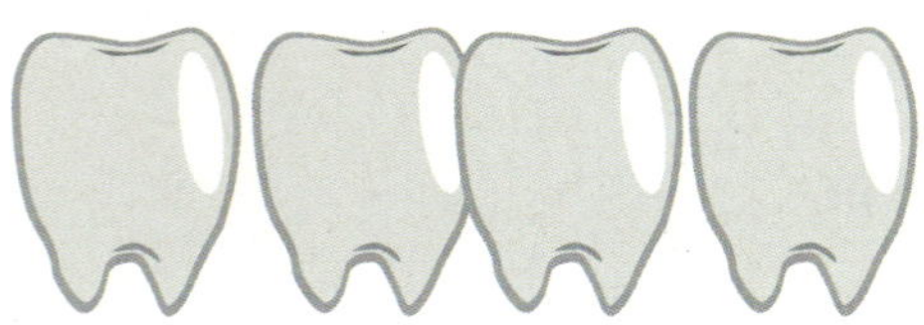	
teeth	

Check out

8 Reading: Children and their health problems

Read the text about the children's problems. Then tick ✓ the correct tip for each of them.

Marietta always stays up late. She watches a lot of video clips on the internet, and she likes playing video games for four or five hours a day. In the morning she is very tired and her head hurts.
Olivia doesn't eat breakfast in the morning. Later at school she gets hungry and thirsty. She can't concentrate during the lessons, and her stomach really hurts.
Pete loves listening to loud music. He also plays the drums and the electric guitar, but he doesn't wear ear protectors. In the evening his ears hurt a lot.
Timothy is a very chatty boy. He likes talking a lot, and he always speaks in a very loud voice. He often gets a sore throat.

1. Marietta shouldn't	☐	be on the internet.	☑	stay up so late.
2. Olivia should	☐	have a healthy breakfast.	☐	eat some snacks.
3. Pete should	☐	turn down the volume.	☐	stop making music.
4. Timothy shouldn't	☐	talk to his friends.	☐	talk all the time.

☺ 😐 ☹ I can understand short texts about health and give advice.
Ich kann kurze Texte über Gesundheit verstehen und dazu Tipps geben.

9 Language in use: Our stomachs hurt!

Match the sentences.

1. Mary's feet hurt.	☐	His dad's head hurts because he always stays up late and watches TV.
2. Joe's fingers hurt.	☐	Their ears hurt because they always listen to loud music.
3. Stephen and Dave's ears hurt.	1	Her feet hurt because she always plays football without shoes.
4. Dario's dad has got a headache.	☐	Our stomachs hurt because we always eat a lot of sweets in the evening.
5. My mum's and my stomachs hurt.	☐	His fingers hurt because he always plays video games and types on his laptop.

☺ 😐 ☹ I can understand and match statements about people's health.
Ich kann Aussagen über Gesundheit verstehen und zuordnen.

☺ = I'm very good at this.
😐 = I can do this.
☹ = I need help.

Doing things around the house

1 What I do at home

4.22 3fv62i

a) **Listen to Patti's audio message to her partner class in Vienna.**

b) **Underline all the things Patti does at home.**

Hi, I am Patti from Chester. Today I want to tell you about my house. Follow me. This is the hall. It's where I take off my shoes. In the kitchen I sometimes cook spaghetti or bake cupcakes. Of course, I do the washing-up, too. I usually have breakfast with my mum here. At weekends Dad comes to visit us. Then we have breakfast and dinner together in the living room. We have a large table with four chairs. It is a huge room with a sofa and two cosy armchairs and a TV. I always watch my favourite shows here. Our bedrooms are upstairs. In my bedroom I do my homework, work on the computer, write text messages and chat with friends. It's my favourite room. This is where I relax and play games – and hide from nosy aunties! The bathroom is on the same floor. It's where I get ready for the day. I always take a shower and brush my teeth. When I leave for school in the morning, I always look at the flowers in the front garden. I often water them and cut the grass. So that's my home. Bye for now and, please, send me a message soon.

c) **Now complete the sentences.**

In the hall she *takes off* 1 her shoes. In the kitchen she sometimes ________ 2 spaghetti or bakes cupcakes. She ________ 3 the washing-up too. She usually ________ 4 breakfast with her mum there.

In the living room she ________ 5 breakfast and dinner with her parents at weekends. She always ________ 6 her favourite TV shows there.

In her bedroom she ________ 7 homework, ________ 8 on the computer, ________ 9 text messages and chats with friends. In her bedroom she ________ 10, plays games and ________ 11 from nosy aunties. In the bathroom she ________ 12 ready for the day. She always ________ 13 a shower and ________ 14 her teeth.

She often ________ 15 the grass and ________ 16 the flowers in the front garden.

Tip

watch → watch**es** relax → relax**es** brush → brush**es**

At home with the Spencer family

2 Vocabulary: Things in the house

Look in these directions: → ↓ ↗

Circle the seven hidden words and write them next to the grid.

	A	B	C	D	E	F	G	H	I	J	K	L
1	T	F	R	I	D	G	E	D	T	L	C	R
2	M	L	C	H	C	N	R	C	Q	Z	I	B
3	I	Q	Z	Y	O	A	Z	T	N	A	Y	A
4	R	C	N	X	O	C	Q	L	H	F	J	T
5	R	Z	Q	B	K	T	Z	C	J	Q	Y	H
6	O	T	P	L	E	Q	M	V	N	C	R	T
7	R	U	H	Y	R	R	T	Z	H	Q	F	U
8	C	T	N	C	A	R	P	E	T	L	Y	B

1. mirror
2.
3.
4.
5.
6.
7.

3 Sarah's message to her sister

Go back to your coursebook p. 75 and read Sarah's e-mail again. Find and underline four more mistakes here. Write the correct sentences below the text.

Hi Sue,
My bedroom is on the ground floor. It is a big room, and I have got my own TV. That's fantastic! Nasreen's room is next to my room. The bathroom is upstairs too. They have a bathtub but no shower. In the living room there is a big green sofa and a huge hi-fi. I like it here.
Love,
Sarah

1. Her bedroom isn't on the ground floor. Her bedroom is upstairs.
2.
3.
4.
5.

4 Writing: My favourite room

Describe your favourite room at home. Use the words below.

cosy | cool | big | nice | tiny | new | dark | friendly | huge

Story time

5 Let's watch Aunt Nancy

4.23 x89xi2

a) Aunt Nancy is back. Sarah and Nasreen are watching her. Listen to what they say.

b) Look at pictures 1–5 and write down what Aunt Nancy is doing in Nasreen's room. Use the verbs below. One verb is wrong.

shake | read | hide | walk | write | ~~open~~

1. *She is opening the door to Nasreen's bedroom.*
2. ______
3. ______
4. ______
5. ______

6 Focus on form: Doing something now

Add *-ing* to the verbs from the green boxes and write them where they belong in the grid below.

~~run~~ | take | sleep | come | watch | sit | chat | dance | sing

		read → reading	hide → hiding	swim → swimming
I	am			*running*
he, she, it	is			
we, you, they	are			

CB p.72

7 Focus on vocabulary: Things in your home

Complete the words from the coursebook p. 72, task 2. The letters in the squares make up the solution.

1. b _ [ ]5 _ _ [ ]11 _
2. _ _ [ ]12 h _ _ [ ]4 _ [ ]6 r
3. [m]1 i c r o w [a]10 v e
4. s _ [ ]3 _
5. _ [ ]2 i [ ]9 _ t
6. _ o _ [ ]8 _ [ ]7

Solution: m _ _ _ _ _ _   _ _ _ _ _

8 Focus on form: What you like doing – What you can do in the house

a) Write at least five different meaningful sentences with the elements given below. Use all the rooms from the grid.

I My sister My brother My mum My dad	like, likes, love, loves, hate, hates, don't, doesn't, can, can't	cook, cooking, do, doing, play, playing, watch, watching, eat, eating	spaghetti, pizza, video games, homework, TV, the washing-up, football	in the kitchen in the bathroom in the bedroom in the hall in the living room

b) Write at least five more sentences in your exercise book.

My brother loves to play ....

Working with words

9 Fiona's room

Look at the picture and write down the words for the things and pieces of furniture.

10 Reading practice

a) Read the text quickly and find out which room it is. Tick ✓ the right box below.

In the middle of the room there is a carpet. There is a mirror on the wall and a tall pot plant next to it. In one corner of the room there is a cosy armchair and a lamp. Between the mirror and the armchair there is a shelf with some books and magazines. The window has got lovely curtains with pink flowers. In front of the window there is a desk with a laptop, a pencil case and some exercise books on it. There is a single bed with some CDs and earphones on it. Above the bed there is a large poster of a famous pop star.

1. bathroom ☐ 2. parents' room ☐ 3. child's room ☐ 4. living room ☐ 5. attic ☐

b) Highlight the words in the text that give you the answer.

Check out

11 What is Aunt Nancy like?

a) Fill in the verbs that tell you what Aunt Nancy *does* or *doesn't do*.

~~want~~ touch play like open look bring

Our Aunt Nancy is a nosy person. She wants 1 to know everything. She ______ 2 into every room. She ______ 3 all the boxes and cupboards. She ______ 4 all our toys. She ______ 5 us sweets. She ______ 6 games with us. She ______ 7 us.

b) Fill in the verbs that tell you what the children *do* or *don't do*.

~~play~~ make like hide want

They sometimes play 1 tricks on her. They ______ 2 funny noises to frighten her. They often ______ 3 in the wardrobe or under the bed. They ______ 4 to see her in their bedrooms. They ______ 5 her at all.

☺ 😐 ☹ I can complete a text about what people usually do and don't do.
Ich kann einen Text über das Verhalten von Menschen vervollständigen.

12 Pippa's room

a) Look at the picture and highlight the six mistakes in the text.

In Pippa's room there is a bed with a cool crocodile on it. She has got a new bathtub in front of the window with a TV and a lamp on her desk. Her schoolbag is under the chair in front of the desk. She has got lots of school things in her room. On the wall there is a lovely poster with a pony in it. There is no carpet, but it is a friendly and very tidy room.

b) Write the correct text in your exercise book.

☺ 😐 ☹ I can compare a text with a picture, and I can correct mistakes.
Ich kann einen Text mit einem Bild vergleichen und Fehler richtigstellen.

☺ = I'm very good at this.
😐 = I can do this.
☹ = I need help.

Unit 10 **Food**

What I eat every day

1 Things to eat and drink

Write the words in the correct box and add *a*, *an* or *some*.

hot chocolate | bacon | toast | bread | ~~pear~~ | ~~orange juice~~ | glass of milk | jam | cornflakes | cup of tea | cup of coffee | sausage | banana | orange | beans | glass of water | apple | tomatoes | egg | bread roll | butter

Food	*a pear,*
Drinks	*some orange juice,*

2 Food and friends

Make a shopping list for your best friend's birthday party. He/she does not eat sweet things. You have got ten pounds to spend.

www.yourpartyfood.co.uk

oranges …… £1.80 per kg
apples …… £2.30 per kg
bananas …… £2.25 per kg

cola …… £1.40 per bottle
lemonade …… £1.60 per bottle

crisps …… £1.90 per bag
chocolates …… £2.70 per box
cake …… £0.65 per piece

Shopping list

It's party time

3 What have we got at home?

Match the phrases with the pictures. Write what the pictures show.

bag of | bottle of | bowl of | box of | can of | cup of | glass of | piece of | slice of | ~~tin of~~

 a tin of baked beans

 ______________

 ______________

 ______________

 ______________

 ______________

 ______________

 ______________

 ______________

 ______________

 ______________

 ______________

4 Asking for something to eat and drink

Complete the sentences. The phrases on the right will help you.

Dialogue 1

A: Can I have **1** baked beans on toast, please?
B: Of course, here you are.
A: Thanks.
B: And what ______ ______ ______ ______ **2** drink?
A: A can of cola, please.

Dialogue 2

C: ______ would you ______ **3** for lunch, George?
D: Some sausages and fried tomatoes, please.

C: Okay, and ______ ______ ______ want ______ **4** drink?
D: I don't know.

C: ______ ______ ______ a glass ______ **5** mineral water?
D: Good idea.

Dialogue 3

E: ______ do you ______ **6** for tea, Patty?

F: Oh, I ______ ______ ______ **7** biscuits and a cup of coffee, please.
E: I'm sorry, there isn't any coffee left.

F: Well, ______ I ______ **8** a hot chocolate instead?
E: Yes, of course.

Useful phrases

Food and drink
- What would you like for … ?
- What would you like to … ?
- Can I have … ?
- What about … ?
- What do you want for … ?
- What do you want to … ?
- Would you like … ?
- Do you want … ?

5 Act it out!

Now write your own dialogue and act it out with a partner in class.

Cooking

6 Fruits and sounds

4.24 b973j3

a) Look at the fruits below and listen to the audio. Say the words.

b) Then write the words next to the pictures.

[p]	peach 		
[b]			
[k]			
[g]			

c) Write other words that start with the same sound in the table above.

7 Reading: Let's make a smoothie!

a) Paul and Kate want to make a smoothie for their friends. In a cookery book they find a recipe. Read the recipe.

Tropical smoothie

Ingredients: *bananas · blueberries · a coconut · a grapefruit · grapes · a teaspoon of honey · a kiwi · some ice cubes · a peach · a pear · a pineapple · a tablespoon of vanilla ice cream*

1. Peel the bananas, the grapefruit, the kiwi, the peach, the pear and the pineapple.
2. Wash the blueberries and the grapes.
3. Ask your parents to open the coconut with a hammer and take out the coconut flesh.
4. Slice the bananas and the kiwi.
5. Cut the coconut, the grapefruit, the peach, the pear and the pineapple into small pieces.
6. Put everything in a blender. Add some ice cubes, a teaspoon of honey and a tablespoon of vanilla ice cream.
7. Blend until smooth.
8. Pour the smoothie into a glass and decorate with fruit pieces.

Turn your smoothie into ice cream! Just put your smoothie in the freezer for an hour to get your own fruit sorbet.

b) What can you do with fruit? Underline the words in the recipe.

c) Now write the words from the recipe next to the fruit.

 peel  ______  ______  ______

8 Writing: Create a fantasy smoothie!

Change three ingredients and write the recipe in your exercise book. Give your smoothie an interesting name.

9 Focus on form: Healthy living

Healthy eating is very important. Make sure you eat the right things at the right time.
Here are some tips for you.

a) Read through this list and ~~cross out~~ the wrong sentences.

1. You should drink a lot when you do sports.
2. You should not stay indoors all day.
3. You should not do sports in your free time.
4. You should play computer games as often as you can.
5. You should not eat too much fat and sugar.
6. You should eat fruit and vegetables four to six times a day.
7. You should not skip breakfast.
8. You should eat as much fish as you can.
9. You should eat junk food.

b) Put the wrong sentences right.

You should ______________________________

____

____

10 Focus on function: Describe your eating habits

a) Read through the questions below and answer them.

- How often do you eat vegetables?
- Do you like meat more than vegetables?
- Do you eat breakfast every day?
- What do you eat for breakfast?
- Do you take a lunch box to school?
- Do you drink juice or water?
- How often do you eat sweets?
- Do you eat a lot in the evening?
- How often do you do sports every week?
- Do you have muesli for breakfast?

b) Now write down your answers in one long text.

____

____

____

____

____

Working with words

11 Word field: Fruit and vegetables

a) Look at the word web FRUIT and add words from the texts in the coursebook and the workbook.

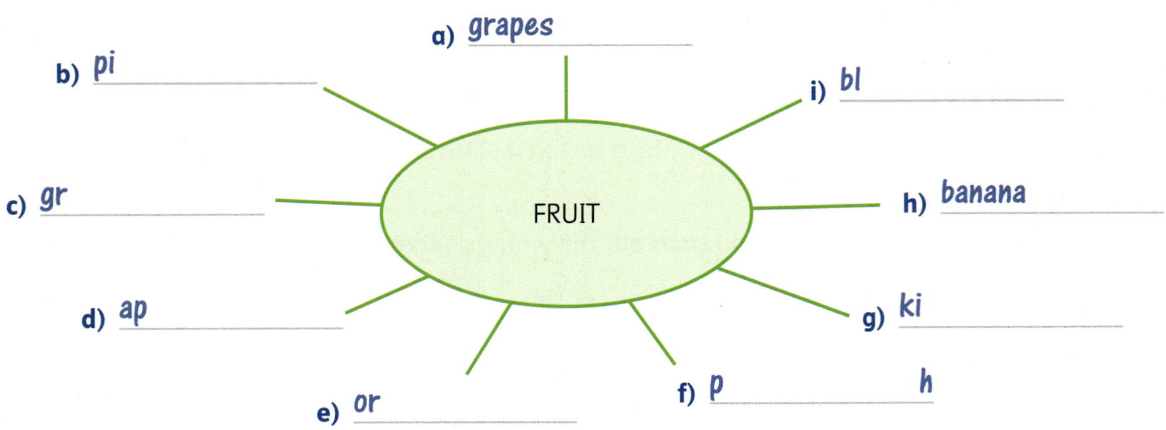

b) Make your own word web about VEGETABLES.

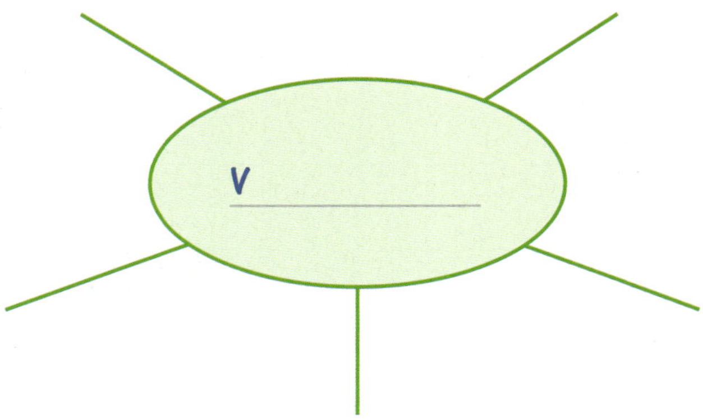

c) Look at the texts in the coursebook again.
Then close the book and write words in the lists. How many can you remember?

Drinks	Sweet things

Check out

12 Reading: What do people eat every day?

a) Read this text about Paula very quickly. What does it tell you? Tick ✓ the correct answer!

- ☐ Paula talks about her school cafeteria and its food.
- ☐ Paula talks about her favourite lunch at school.
- ☐ Paula talks about the food she eats for breakfast, lunch and dinner.

My name is Paula, and I am from Manchester, England. For breakfast I sometimes have a bowl of cornflakes with milk, and I always drink a glass of orange juice. School starts at half past eight, and in my first break I often eat a piece of fruit. I always have lunch in our school cafeteria. The food there is really good, and I love the dish of the day, but I also like the school cafeteria's snacks. I usually eat some salad and some hot food like pasta, lasagna or chicken curry. I never eat dessert because I don't like sweet things. I sometimes have a pear or a banana, but I never eat cake or muffins. School ends at five o'clock in the afternoon and I get home at half past six. My dad always cooks dinner. First, we eat some salad. Then we eat something hot. We often have fish and vegetables. I love vegetables and my favourite vegetable is broccoli. Sometimes we have dessert, too, like fruit salad. It's yummy.

☺ 😐 ☹ I can understand the main idea of a text.
Ich kann das Thema eines Texts verstehen.

**b) Read the text again and check the statements.
Tick ✓ T (= true) or F (= false).**

		T (true)	F (false)
1.	Paula skips breakfast in the morning.	☐	✓
2.	She always has lunch in the school cafeteria.	☐	☐
3.	For lunch she has some salad and also some hot food like pasta.	☐	☐
4.	Paula cooks dinner for her mum and dad.	☐	☐
5.	She loves vegetables, but she doesn't like broccoli.	☐	☐

☺ 😐 ☹ I can find detailed information in a text.
Ich kann Details aus einem Text entnehmen.

c) Tina describes what she eats every day. Fill the gaps with words from the text above.

Hi, I'm Tina. I always eat muesli for *breakfast* 1. Sometimes I drink a ________ 2 of orange juice. I go to school from 8.15 a.m. to 4 p.m. and in the first break I eat a piece of ________ 3 like an apple or a banana. At 1.30 p.m. I have lunch in our school ________ 4. I usually eat the ________ 5 of the day. I don't eat ________ 6 because I don't like sweet food like muffins or cupcakes. When I get home in the late afternoon, my parents cook ________ 7.

☺ 😐 ☹ I can complete short texts about food.
Ich kann kurze Texte über Essen vervollständigen.

☺ = I'm very good at this.
😐 = I can do this.
☹ = I need help.

Talking about the weather

1 If it's raining ...

a) Do the crossword below and find the magic word. Then match the pictures with the answers from the crossword and write the numbers.

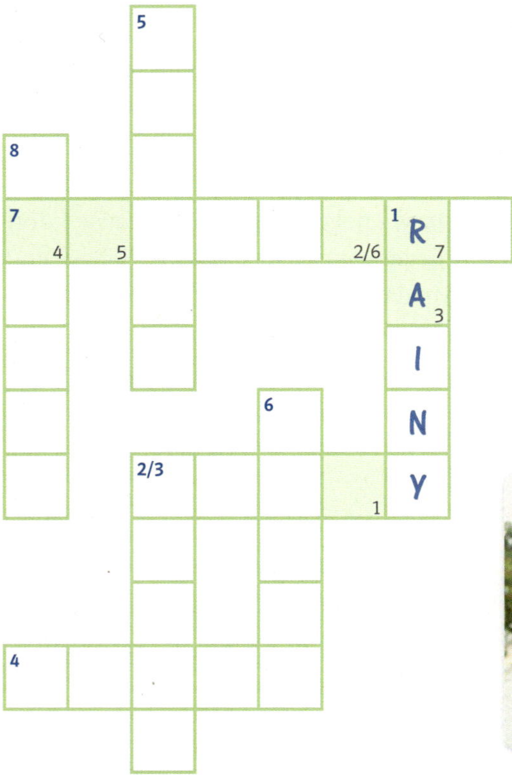

1. It's raining. = It's rainy.
2. It's snowing. = It's ...
3. The sun is shining. = It's ...
4. The wind is blowing. = It's ...
5. There are many clouds in the sky. = It's ...
6. There's a lot of fog. = It's ...
7. There's a thunderstorm. = It's ...
8. There's a storm. = It's ...

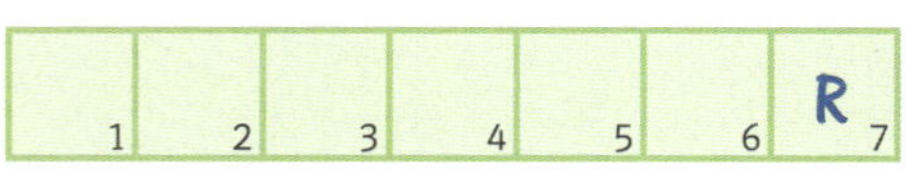

b) Read the statements about the weather in Austria. Tick ✓ T (= true) or F (= false).

	T (true)	F (false)
1. In Austria winters are usually cold, snowy and trees have no leaves.	✓	
2. Summer isn't very warm or sunny, and you can't go swimming.		
3. Spring and autumn are good times for planting new flowers.		
4. It's usually foggy and cloudy in autumn; for example in November.		
5. There's usually no snow to go skiing or snowboarding in winter.		

c) **Write a short text about the weather in Austria (around 50 words). Use at least four words from the green box and answer the questions below:**

cold • windy • season • month • cloudy • friends • hot • summer • rain

- What's your favourite season/month? Why?
- What's the weather like in winter?
- What's the weather like in summer?
- Which activities do you do if it's hot/cold outside?
- What kind of weather don't you like? Why?

2 What will the weather be like tomorrow?

a) **Look at this weather forecast. Then match the pictures with the statements below.**

A ◯

4 p.m. – 10 p.m.

B ◯

9 a.m. – 11 a.m.

C ◯

11 a.m. – 4 p.m.

D ◯

5 a.m. – 8 a.m.

1. In the morning from 5 a.m. to 8 a.m. there will be rain and it will be stormy. It will be chilly outside, temperatures will be around 9 °C.
2. It will be cloudy and a bit windy, but the sun will shine. We will have temperatures of around 16 °C.
3. From 11 a.m. to 4 p.m. the sun will shine. There will be a few clouds, but it will be warm at 22 °C.
4. In the late afternoon it will be very sunny and hot. Temperatures will be around 28 °C.

b) **Jumbled sentences: Put the words in the correct order.**

1. rainy • Tomorrow • will • be • it • cloudy • and

Tomorrow it will be rainy and cloudy.

2. it • will • snow • in • Tomorrow • afternoon • the

____

3. there • thunderstorm • be • will • a • at • night • Tomorrow

____

4. sunny • hot • and • will • it • be • Tomorrow • all • day • long

____

The weather around the year

3 The months of the year

Fill in the missing letters. Then match the sentence halves and write the numbers and words.

1. J a n u a r y		is the fourth month of the year.
2. _ e b _ u a r y	7	is the ______ month of the year.
3. M _ r _ h	11	is the ______ month of the year.
4. A _ r _ l	1	is the first month of the year.
5. _ a y		is the tenth month of the year.
6. J u n _	3	is the ______ month of the year.
7. J _ l _	9	is the ______ month of the year.
8. A u _ u _ t		is the twelfth month of the year.
9. S _ p _ e m b e r		is the second month of the year.
10. _ c t o _ e r	5	is the ______ month of the year.
11. N o _ e _ b e _		is the eighth month of the year.
12. D e _ e m _ e r		is the sixth month of the year.

4 Clara and the weather

Read the text about Clara and her family. Fill in the words from the box.

~~winter~~ • cold • windy • summer
autumn • sunny • spring • cloudy

My favourite season is winter **1**. In winter it's usually very ______ **2** and we can go skiing, but last year winter was really bad. It was very foggy and rainy. My dad's favourite season is ______ **3** because he loves planting new flowers. He doesn't like it when it's ______ **4** because the wind ruins all his flowers. My mum's favourite season is ______ **5** because she loves the hot and ______ **6** weather.

My brother's favourite season is ______ **7** because he likes to see the leaves falling from the trees. Well, I don't like that. I think ______ **8** weather is horrible.

Talking about now and then

5 Focus on form: Is it raining?

Match the questions with the answers. Then complete the missing verbs.

1. Is it raining, John? ☐ Yes, the sun is ____________ . It's really hot.
2. Lisa, is it snowing? ☐ 1 Yes, it is. It's raining quite a lot, and it's cold.
3. Is the sun shining? ☐ No, the wind isn't ____________ .
4. Is the wind blowing, Linda? ☐ No, it isn't ____________ . It's too warm.

6 Focus on form: Last weekend

Use the words on the right and complete the text. went | were | went | ~~made~~ | was | were

Last Saturday my sister Anabel made 1 our favourite chocolate cake with strawberries and blueberries. In the afternoon my mum and dad, my two sisters, my younger brother and I ____________ 2 to a very nice park. It ____________ 3 warm and sunny. There ____________ 4 no clouds in the sky, and we had about 28 °C. We played badminton and volleyball. At four we ____________ 5 really hungry and so we ate a lot of Anabel's cake. Around 5 p.m. we ____________ 6 back home.

7 Focus on form: Crazy weather

Read the story "Crazy weather" (→ coursebook p. 92) again. Then complete the summary with the correct tense (present progressive / past simple).

It's a sunny afternoon. There's no wind, and Granny is sitting 1 outside in her armchair. She ____________ 2 her grandchildren playing in the garden. Suddenly she shouts, "Look, the forsythia ____________ 3 ! That's crazy." Her granddaughter Clare asks, "Granny, why ______ you ____________ 4 your head?" Granny says, "This weather is crazy. When I ______ 5 a girl like you, winters ______ 6 a bit different. It ______ 7 cold and freezing." "I see," Clare says. Granny goes on and says, "And there ______ 8 a lot of snow. There ______ 9 no flowers at this time of the year." "Well," says Clare, "I like warm winters more than cold ones."

Working with words

8 How to practise vocabulary

a) **Look at the grid below and write five more (new) words. What other words come to your mind when you read the words "weather", "months" and "ordinal numbers"? How long does it take you to complete the grid? Use your phone and see how much time you need.**

WEATHER	MONTHS	ORDINAL NUMBERS
rain	*May*	*third*
Time: ____________ seconds	Time: ____________ seconds	Time: ____________ seconds

b) **Now check the words in your coursebook (→ coursebook p. 87 and vocabulary p. 170) and make sure your words in the grid are correct. How many words are correct?**

15–14: Excellent ☺ ☺
13–12: Good work ☺
11–10: Okay! 😐
9–8: You need to practise more ☹
7–0: Do this exercise one more time ☹ ☹

My score is: ____________

c) **Look at the word below. Think of one more word for each letter of the word "weather". If you want to, you can use the vocabulary list in your coursebook.**

S
E

W	E	A	T	H	E	R

S
O
N

Check out

9 Language in use: Be a weather expert

Match the sentence halves.

1. If it's cloudy,	☐	we call them spring, summer, autumn and winter.
2. Temperatures in summer	☐	says what the weather will be like in the future.
3. Rain is water	☐	can be very high at around 35 °C.
4. There are four seasons;	☐	that falls from the sky.
5. A weather forecast	1	there are many clouds in the sky.

☺ 😐 ☹ I can understand statements about the weather.
Ich kann Beschreibungen zum Thema Wetter verstehen.

10 Reading: The weather in Australia

Read Karin's blog about the weather in Australia. Then tick ✓ T (= true) or F (= false).

From: AustralianGirl

The weather in my country
Hey guys,
Last time my blog was about the food in Australia. Today I'm telling you about the weather in my country. You know, Australia is an island, and it's also a continent. In summer it's usually very hot, and in winter it isn't too cold. In summer it's also very dry here, and sometimes it can be quite stormy. It doesn't rain very often, so water is special to us. And there's no snow in Australia.
Alright then … greetings from Australia ☺

Internet 100 %

	T (true)	F (false)
1. In Australia it's warm and sunny, but it isn't very hot and dry.	☐	✓
2. Australia is an island, but it isn't a continent.	☐	☐
3. It can also be stormy every now and then.	☐	☐
4. Rain is nothing special because it often rains.	☐	☐
5. In Australia it usually doesn't snow.	☐	☐

☺ 😐 ☹ I can understand short texts about the weather in other countries.
Ich kann kurze Texte über das Wetter in anderen Ländern verstehen.

☺ = I'm very good at this.
😐 = I can do this.
☹ = I need help.

Unit 12 Adventure in Grumpland – a play

1 Words from the play

a) Highlight four more adjectives green and highlight four more nouns yellow in the grid below.

b) Write them in the right boxes below the picture and match them with each other. → ↓ ↗ ↘ ↙

	A	B	C	D	E	F	G	H	I	J	K	L
1	U	N	P	Z	W	Y	G	R	U	M	P	Y
2	G	F	J	H	C	M	F	F	F	D	C	H
3	L	B	C	I	Z	O	M	M	D	A	R	K
4	T	N	G	H	R	X	Y	Y	K	Q	Y	Z
5	Y	A	T	E	L	Y	W	I	T	C	H	R
6	M	H	S	Q	J	P	K	L	H	Z	D	F
7	F	T	T	V	T	H	O	J	Z	Y	V	R
8	R	B	N	V	H	W	G	T	B	N	F	U
9	K	I	N	G	V	C	W	P	I	Z	X	I
10	Q	T	R	F	F	B	H	F	C	O	H	T
11	D	E	L	I	C	I	O	U	S	L	N	R

	Adjectives	Nouns
1.	*grumpy*	*King*
2.		
3.		
4.		
5.		

c) Which words go together? Put a cross (X) in the right boxes.

	cold	old	hungry	lovely	sweet	magic	dark	ugly
wand						X		
cabbage								
castle								
wizard								
prison								
children								

d) Write them in your exercise book.

a magic wand, …

2 Focus on form: An interview after the adventure

a) Write Rory's answers. Use the words below.

was | wasn't | were | weren't

Interviewer: Why did you not find your way back?

Rory: There were [1] so many trees.

It ____ [2] a very dark forest.

Interviewer: How did you get to Grumpland?

Rory: I don't know. Suddenly there ____ [3] this castle. It ____ [4] there before.

Interviewer: Strange. And then someone came out from behind a tree, right?

Rory: Yes, it ____ [5] Kip. He ____ [6] collecting wood for the King.

Interviewer: He saw you were holding some fruit in your hands. What did he say about this fruit?

Rory: He told us it ____ [7] only for the King to eat. He said we ____ [8] allowed to eat it.

Interviewer: What happened next?

Rory: Then there ____ [9] the sound of a whistle and all of a sudden all the King's Guards ____ [10] standing around us. …

4.25 5f788j

b) Now listen and check your answers.

3 How we met King Grump

a) Some days later Lucy writes about their adventure for the school magazine. Read this part of Lucy's text and highlight the verbs in the past form.

We lost our way in a dark forest. All the trees had strange faces. Their fruit looked like orange and blue footballs. Rory picked a fruit because he wanted to taste it. But then the King's Guards came. They told us that only the King was allowed to eat this jub-jub fruit, and they took us to the castle. The King was very grumpy because he had a stomach problem. When he ate the fruit, he got terrible hiccups. Nobody could cure him. He sent us to prison. There we met a witch and a wizard. They said that the only way to get out of prison was to find a cure for the King's hiccups. …

b) **Match the verbs in Lucy's text with their base forms in the grid below.**

base form	past form
lose	lost
pick	
want	
come	
eat	

base form	past form
have	
be	
tell	
get	
say	

base form	past form
look	
take	
meet	
send	
can	

4 More questions about the adventure

The following interview got jumbled up. Put it right and match the questions with the answers.

Questions		Answers
1. Why did you pick the jub-jub fruit, Rory?	☐	He put us in prison.
2. Why did the Guards take you to the King?	☐	Yes, he did. He ate jub-jub fruit.
3. Did the King welcome you?	☐	They ate only cabbage and turnips.
4. Did he have lunch?	☐	Sam tried to text his parents.
5. What did the King's people eat?	1	Because I wanted to taste it.
6. Where did the King put you?	☐	Because we had the fruit in our hands.
7. What did you do to get help?	☐	No, he didn't. He was a grumpy old man.

5 Word order

Put the words in the right order to make correct sentences.

1. meet • the children • the witch and wizard • in the garden • didn't

   The children didn't meet the witch and wizard in the garden.

2. didn't • jub-jub fruit • eat • the Queen ______________________.
3. of that • didn't • we • think • why ______________________?
4. did • he • say • what ______________________?

6 Focus on form: Weird recipes

In Grumpland – now Jub-Jub Land – the people are making up all sorts of recipes with the different fruits in their country. Here is one of their favourites.

a) How to make turnip shakes. Read the recipe and fill in the correct word.

Turnip shake

Get 1 (teg) a turnip and ______ 2 (lepe) it.

______ 3 (uct) it into cubes.

______ 4 (ktae) an onion and ______ 5 (icels) it thinly.

______ 6 (thea) a tablespoon of butter and a teaspoon of olive oil in a pan.

______ 7 (tup) the turnip and the onion in the pan and ______ 8 (yrf) them until they are soft.

______ 9 (nebld) the cooked vegetables with two cups of cabbage ice cream.

______ 10 (sirt) until creamy.

______ 11 (dad) four teaspoons of honey, a little pepper and a pinch of salt.

b) What do you think of this recipe? What is it like? Write down what you think.

I think	the turnip shake	is	okay delicious horrible strange	because	it's too sweet, salty, … (for me, for my taste) it's boring, interesting, strange … . it's a bit, very … . there's too much … in it.

c) Now write your recipe for a cool fantasy drink. Draw a picture of it for a cookery book and colour it nicely.

Check out

7 Who says what in the play?

Pick from the green boxes. There is one person too many.

Wizard | Pembridge | Lucy | Chief Guard | ~~King~~ | Kip

1. King : "Put them in prison."
2. ______ : "I'm collecting wood for the King."
3. ______ : "What do I do with these strange children?"
4. ______ : "There's no signal in Grumpland."
5. ______ : "It didn't work."

☺ 😐 ☹ I can match speakers with their statements.
Ich kann Aussagen Personen zuordnen.

8 Cures that didn't work

Sam writes about Jemma and Rory's cures. Complete his text with the correct forms. There is one word too many.

~~is / was~~ | is / was (3x) | goes / went | closes / closed | stands / stood | takes / took (2x) | says / said | drinks / drank | doesn't / didn't | cannot / couldn't (2x) | puts / put | like / liked | sits / sat | opens / opened

One cure was 1 this: The King ______ 2 his eyes. The lights ______ 3 out. It ______ 4 very dark. Rory ______ 5 behind the King. The King ______ 6 his eyes, but he ______ 7 see anybody. Suddenly, Rory ______ 8 "BOO!" behind him. It ______ 9 so funny. It ______ 10 work, but I ______ 11 it a lot.

The other cure ______ 12 this: The King ______ 13 a glass of water and ______ 14 down. He ______ 15 off his crown and ______ 16 his head between his knees. Then he tried to drink the water, but he ______ 17 .

☺ 😐 ☹ I can complete a short text about the past.
Ich kann einen kurzen Text über Vergangenes vervollständigen.

☺ = I'm very good at this.
😐 = I can do this.
☹ = I need help.

Birthdays

Unit 13

A very special birthday party

1 Granny Camilla's birthday party

Complete the dialogue and put in the missing sentences. There are three sentences too many.

- Alright. Did you have a nice weekend?
- Did you text her?
- She wanted to have a photo album of the whole family.
- Yes, we did. My mum went to a shop in town and bought a very nice album for her.
- And what did she give you?
- ~~Hi Susanna, how are you?~~
- Yes, she was really excited.
- Oh, no. There was my elder brother, my uncle and my aunt and my two cousins.
- My weekend was really nice.
- Was the weather nice?
- Yes, we celebrated my grandmother's 75th birthday.
- We had lunch in the garden and then we had a little party in the evening.

Tom: 1. *Hi Susanna, how are you?*

Susanna: Thanks, I'm fine. And you?

Tom: 2. ____________________

Susanna: No, not really, it was boring. There was nothing to do and the weather was awful.

Tom: 3. ____________________

Susanna: Oh, was it?

Tom: 4. ____________________
She looked so happy. It was such a nice day. Everybody had a good time.

Susanna: Was it just you and your parents?

Tom: 5. ____________________
And of course, granddad. And we also invited some of her best friends.

Susanna: And what did you do?

Tom: 6. ____________________
It was really nice because everybody helped. My uncle made a carrot cake, and my brother and I – we helped with the drinks. And we played her favourite music.

Susanna: And what did she get?

Tom: 7. ____________________

Susanna: And did you get one for her?

Tom: 8. ____________________
We wanted to make this a really nice birthday for her. We also took a lot of pictures.

Susanna: How nice!

Tom: 9. ____________________
She looked very elegant in her new dress. And she was smiling all the time. Sweet.

Camilla's birthday party

2 Reading: Fiona Brown tells a lie to her mum

a) Read the dialogue about Granny Camilla's birthday party in task 1 again. In the evening Fiona Brown came home and chatted with her mother on the phone about her day.

Hi Fiona, how was your day?

It was great. I went to Camilla's birthday party. It was really sweet.

Great! Did she get a nice birthday cake?

Yep, the cake was lovely – it was a cheese cake. Grandpa made it for her ☺

Wow …! Did she get many presents?

Yeah. The best one was a little kitten ☺ ☺ ☺

And did she like it?

No, she didn't. She looked really stressed.

Why?

You know … Granny doesn't like cats!!!

Hmmm … Did she keep it then?

No. she didn't. I took the cat. Now we've got a little kitten. Isn't that cool?

b) Read the chat again and find the three lies and write down the correct sentences.

1. ______________________

2. ______________________

3. ______________________

c) Why do you think Fiona lied to her mother? Tick ✓ the right answer.

- ☐ Because she wanted to have a cat.
- ☐ Because she wanted a nice cake for her birthday.
- ☐ Because she hated cats.
- ☐ Because she wanted to play a trick on her mum.

3 Focus on form: Past tense forms

took bought came

~~said~~ gave saw made sang

a) Irregular forms: Find the right pairs.

Present tense	Past tense	Present tense	Past tense
say	said	sing	
come		buy	
give		make	
take		see	

b) Go back to the stories in your coursebook and find three sentences with irregular forms. Then write them in the space below or in your exercise book.

1. ______________________________________

2. ______________________________________

3. ______________________________________

c) Regular forms: Complete the table.

Present tense	Past tense	Present tense	Past tense
arrive	arrived	organise	
play		prepare	
check		watch	
celebrate		help	

4 Hi Clara, how was the party?

Read the dialogue and fill in the right forms of the past tense.

Ben: Hi Clara, tell me about Christopher's party at the weekend.

Clara: Hi Ben, it ___was___ 1 (be) awful. There ______ 2 (be) a lot of people, but the music ______ 3 (be) really bad.

Ben: Who else was there?

Clara: There ______ 4 (be) some of my friends from school but they ______ 5 (not, talk) to me. They only ______ 6 (talk) to each other.

Ben: Did you bring a present?

Clara: Yes, I did, but I don't think Christopher ______ 7 (like) it. He said "Thank you," but he ______ 8 (not, smile).

Ben: Was Robin there as well?

Clara: No, he ______ 9 (not, come). He ______ 10 (be) ill and had to stay in bed.

Ben: So the party ______ 11 (be) really boring for you?

Clara: Yes, that's right. That was the reason I ______ 12 (not, stay) very long.

Ben: And did you go home straight away?

Clara: No, I didn't. I ______ 13 (get) a message from my friends, and so I ______ 14 (play) volleyball with them in the park. That ______ 15 (be) nice. – And what did you do?

Ben: I ______ 16 (not, do) much. I ______ 17 (stay) at home, and I ______ 18 (want) to help my mum in the garden. But then my granny ______ 19 (call) me on my mobile, and so I ______ 20 (go) to see her. That was all I did.

Working with words

5 Learning new words: Birthday activities

a) Study the words and pictures carefully.

get/give presents

have a party

decorate a room

visit family and friends

eat special food / have your favourite meal

go to a restaurant

give/get cards or invitations

make/eat a cake

play games

dance a lot

sing "Happy Birthday"

wear new clothes / wear something special

b) Cover up the box above and say the words.

1

2

3

4

5

6

7

8

9

10

11

12

Check out

6 This was my birthday party

call | celebrate | get | give | have | help | make | ~~is~~ | post | sing | start | text | want

Fill in the correct forms of the past tense.

My last birthday was 1 great. I ______ 2 a lot of presents from my friends and from my family. And I ______ 3 a great party. The week before the party I ______ 4 invitations to some of my friends, and I ______ 5 some others on their mobiles. Everybody ______ 6 to come. We ______ 7 my birthday at home. My parents ______ 8 me to decorate the living room with balloons. And my mum ______ 9 cupcakes for everybody. It ______ 10 at three o'clock in the afternoon. But the best moment was when my parents ______ 11 me a little puppy. I was so happy that I ______ 12 my grandma to tell her all about him. His name is Brooklyn. He is so sweet. And then everyone ______ 13 "Happy Birthday" – a perfect day.

☺ 😐 ☹ I can complete short texts in the past tense.
Ich kann kurze Texte in der Past tense vervollständigen.

7 Past tense questions and negations

Make questions and answers.

1. Did they all sing "Happy Birthday"? – No, they did not. They didn't sing "Happy Birthday".
2. What did you get for your birthday?

   I • a new mobile • get ______
3. make • your grandma • cake • for you • ? ______
   No, she didn't. She didn't have time.
4. Did you see your father at the weekend?

   No, I didn't. time • not • have • he ______
5. What • give • her • you • as • a present • ? ______
   I gave her a new book on her favourite band.

☺ 😐 ☹ I can form questions and negative sentences in the past tense.
Ich kann Fragen und verneinte Sätze in der Past tense bilden.

☺ = I'm very good at this.
😐 = I can do this.
☹ = I need help.

Taking care of pets

1 Listening: How kids look after their pets

4.26 rp7z8t

Listen to the children and write down their pets.

1. Lisa has got a ___*dog*___ .
2. Dan has got a __________ .
3. Chris has got a __________ .
4. Joe has got some __________ .
5. Sue has got a __________ .
6. Diane has got a __________ .

2 What's the vet's advice?

a) Choose the vet's advice for the animals' problems.

problems	advice
My cat, Fridolin, has stomach ache. My dog, Penny, is too fat. Fritzi, my guinea pig, has itchy skin. Tristan, my budgie, doesn't sing. My hippo Bertha smells.	brush her/his fur once a week clean her/his food tray every day don't feed her/him hot dogs or cake walk her/him three times a day don't give her/him any milk to drink bathe her/him get a second pet as a friend for her/him brush her/his teeth twice a day

b) Look at the example and write the vet's advice in your exercise book.

You should clean Fridolin's food tray every day. You shouldn't feed him hot dogs and cake. You shouldn't give him any milk to drink.

CB p.115

A new home

3 Fluffy's daily routine

a) Read the interview in unit 14 again (→ coursebook p. 115). Find five more mistakes in this text and highlight them.

Two years ago Fluffy's home was an animal shelter. Now Fluffy lives with the Webber family. He thinks they take good care of him. And this is his daily routine:

In the morning he stretches his legs before he gets his food. Then Alex often takes Fluffy to the swimming pool and brushes his teeth. When the boys are at school, Fluffy watches the neighbour's cats. After school the boys usually play with Fluffy for about an hour. Then it's homework time for George, Fluffy and Alex. In the evening Mr Webber and Fluffy usually go for a walk.

Fluffy is very happy with the Webber family.

b) Now correct the wrong sentences. Use negations.

1. *Fluffy doesn't stretch his legs before he gets his food in the morning.*
2. ______
3. ______
4. ______
5. ______
6. ______

4 Scrambled animals

a) Unscramble the animal words.

1. samlina *a n i m a l s* (1)
2. shroe _ _ _ _ [4]
3. knaes _ _ _ [3] _
4. bibrat _ _ _ _ [2] _
5. netikt _ _ _ _ [8] _
6. upypp _ _ [7] _ [6]
7. eusmo [5] _ _ _ _

b) Look at task 4a. The letters in the squares make up a sentence. Write down the solution.

Solution: I *l* ___ ___ ___ ___ ___ ___ ___ t.

Talking animals

5 A story: The lion and the mouse

Complete the story and use the words from the boxes below.

~~was~~ | jumped | saw | came | said (3x) | smiled
wanted | liked | started | opened | looked (2x)

One day Leo, the Great Lion, ___was___ 1 sleeping under a tree.

Along __________ 2 a little mouse and __________ 3 up the Lion's nose. At that moment the Lion __________ 4 his eyes and __________ 5 to eat him. But the mouse __________ 6, "Sorry, Great Lion. I'm not good food for a great King like you. Let me go and I'll never forget this all my life."

The Great Lion __________ 7 these sweet words and let the mouse go.

A day later the little mouse __________ 8 Leo, the Great Lion, with thick ropes all around his body. The King's Guards wanted to take him to their King.

"Oh, now I can keep my word", the mouse __________ 9 and __________ 10 to bite away the ropes. The Lion __________ 11 down at the little helper and __________ 12. The little mouse __________ 13 up at the Great Lion and __________ 14, "Little friends can be great friends."

6 Focus on form: Asking for information

Work with a partner. Choose Text A or B. Cover up the other text. Ask your partner questions to complete your text. Take turns.

A My pet

My birthday was on 6th April **1**. My parents gave me a guinea pig. It was a big surprise. Maggie is 10 months old. Her coat is ________ **2**. She lives in a large box with a lot of dry grass. In one corner of her box there is a little bowl of water. She needs ________ **3** every day. Next to the bowl there is a ________ **4**. She eats lettuce, carrots and dry bread. When I come home from school Maggie says ________ **5** in her language, which sounds like "Squeak, squeak". I take her out of her box and let her run up and down in my room. Sometimes she just sits on ________ **6**. She is such a lovely pet. I love her a lot.

Student A: When was your birthday? **Student B:** On 6th April. *(Student A fills the gap.)*

B My pet

My birthday was on 6th April. My parents gave me a guinea pig **1**. It was a big surprise. Maggie is ________ **2** old. Her coat is white and brown. She lives in ________ **3** with a lot of dry grass. In one corner of her box there is a little ________ **4**. She needs fresh water every day. Next to the bowl there is a small plate for her food. She eats ________ **5**.When I come home from school Maggie says "Hello" to me in her language, which sounds like "Squeak, squeak". I take her out of her box and let her run up and down ________ **6**. Sometimes she just sits on my knees. She is such a lovely pet. I love her a lot.

Student B: What did your parents give you? **Student A:** A guinea pig. *(Student B fills the gap.)*

Working with words

7 Animals around the world

Study the picture and the word list. Circle the words with the colour of the continent.

bear bird camel chameleon crocodile fish elephant flamingo giraffe

gorilla horse lion monkey mouse/mice panda parrot

penguin raccoon snake seal tiger zebra

Check out

What (crossed out) · Who · Why · What (3x) · Where · Did

8 Asking questions

4.27 35gd4a

Complete the dialogue with the correct question starters. Use the words from the green boxes. There is one word too many. Then listen and check.

David: Granny, Granny! We've got a pet.

Granny: Really? What 1 is it?
David: It's a dog.

Granny: ____ 2 did you get it from?
David: From the Animal Shelter in Bakersville.

Granny: I see. ____ 3 other animals were there?
David: Oh, there were lots of other animals. Guinea pigs, budgies, hamsters …

Granny: Ah, but ____ 4 did you take a dog?
David: Well, because a dog is a fine pet, isn't it?

Granny: ____ 5 you all want to have a dog?
David: Well, no, we didn't. But Dad … hmm.

Granny: Yes? ____ 6 about Dad?
David: Well, the dog ran over to him and then Dad felt something warm on his leg.

Granny: Something warm? ____ 7 was it?
David: It peed on him!
Granny: Oh, I like that.

☺ 😐 ☹ I can ask questions about a past event.
Ich kann Fragen über ein vergangenes Ereignis stellen.

9 Getting it right: Put the words in the right order

1. always • on a lead • Sharon • her puppy • keeps

   Sharon always keeps her puppy on a lead.

2. an • ago • the Webbers • shelter • two • visited • animal • years

   ____

3. see • you • exotic • zoo • animals • can • lots of • the • at

   ____

4. my • sick, • when • rat • pet • was • vet • I • the • took • him • to

   ____

5. should • keep • you • your • of • cage • clean • budgie • always • the

   ____

☺ 😐 ☹ I can put words in the correct order.
Ich kann Wörter zu einem richtigen Satz zusammenfügen.

☺ = I'm very good at this.
😐 = I can do this.
☹ = I need help.

Going on holiday

Unit 15

Holiday habits

1 Listening: Holidays are fun!

4.28 8v4rk4

a) Listen to the children and circle the mistakes. There are three mistakes in each text.

Children and their holiday habits

1. MELISSA – Hey there, my name is Melissa and in summer I usually go hiking with my grandparents. Last year, we went to the mountains in Carinthia. My uncle loves being active and doing outdoor activities like hiking. I like being outside too, especially if it rains. What I like best is taking photos of animals and eating berries we pick in the woods.

2. RUSSEL – Hi, I'm Russel and I love the summer holidays because I can relax and hang out with my friends. My best friend Djordje and I never go away on holiday because we love staying home. We play a lot of football. In the morning we always go to the park because there is nobody else around at the football field, and in the afternoon we play virtual football on Djordje's PlayStation.

3. AGNES – Hey, my name is Agnes. For our summer holiday my mum and I always go on a city trip because my dad loves sightseeing. Last year we went to Rome. It was absolutely great. When I'm on holiday, I always read a lot of books. In Rome we saw many interesting sights: the Colosseum, the Trevi Fountain and of course the Vatican. On our last day, we had the best pizza ever at Piazza Navona.

4. MARTIN – Hello, I'm Martin. I love the summer holidays because my family and I usually go to the sea. It is really cool to play on the beach or try out surfing in the sea. My favourite beach is in Croatia, but this year we are going to fly to Greece. We are a big family: me, my mum and my dad and also my step-sister. She is my dad's daughter. We also have a cat, but she doesn't like travelling, so she is going to stay at home this year.

b) Correct the mistakes and write the sentences in your exercise book.

Hey there, my name is Melissa and in summer I usually go hiking with my uncle and aunt.

CB p.122

2 Plans for our holiday

Go back to Stephen and Tina (→ coursebook p. 122, task 4b) and complete the questions and answers below.

do | stay (2x) | ~~fly~~ | fly | travel | take | meet

1. Stephen, are you *going to fly* to Germany in the holidays? – *Yes, I am.*
2. Are you ______ for eight days? – ______
3. Are you ______ to Berlin? – ______
4. Are you ______ a lot of sightseeing? – ______
5. Tina, are you ______ to New Zealand? – ______
6. Are you ______ for one month? – ______
7. Are you ______ the plane? – ______
8. Are you ______ some friends? – ______

3 Doing a lot of stuff

Write down what Shania is going to do and what she isn't going to do in the school holidays.

1. *I'm going to cook pizza.*

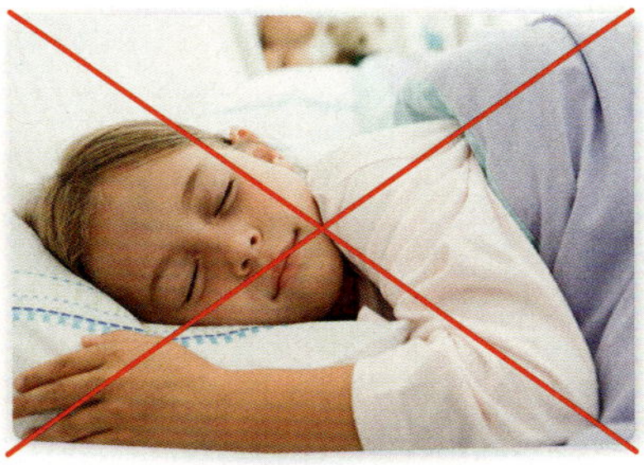

2. ______

3. ______

4. ______

5. ______

6. ______

Hooray – holiday!

4 Holiday master plan

Go back to the song "Holiday master plan" (→ coursebook p. 124). What do the pictures below have to do with the song? Write the lines from the song under the pictures.

1. play games on the screen
2. ______
3. ______
4. ______

5 Writing: My holidays

Use the grid below to write a short text for your school magazine about your summer holidays.

<table>
<tr><td>Who are you?</td><td colspan="4">My name is … ./I'm … .</td></tr>
<tr><td>What do you usually do?</td><td>In the summer holidays
I love the holidays because
In the summer</td><td rowspan="2">I
we
my mum and I
my family and I
my grandparents and I
…</td><td>always
usually
sometimes</td><td rowspan="2">play on the beach.
hang out with friends.
visit a theme park.
stay at a farm.
join a summer camp.
play board games.
…</td></tr>
<tr><td>What are you going to do this year?</td><td>This year,
This summer,</td><td>am going to
are going to</td></tr>
<tr><td>Where are you going?</td><td></td><td rowspan="2">I
We
My mum and I
My family and I
My grandparents and I</td><td>am going to
are going to</td><td>travel to London by car.
fly to Greece.
visit Italy by ship.
stay at home.
visit relatives/friends.
…</td></tr>
<tr><td>What are you going to do there?</td><td></td><td>am going to
are going to</td><td>take a lot of photos.
buy souvenirs.
read a good book.
do some sightseeing.
swim in the sea.
build sandcastles.
sleep all day long.
…</td></tr>
</table>

Talking about the past

~~be~~ | be (2x) | do | go (3x) | grill | have | show | stay | taste | watch

6 Focus on form: My favourite holiday

Karam writes about his favourite holiday. Complete the text.

My favourite holiday *was* 1 when we ______ 2 to Australia. We ______ 3 there for one month. I ______ 4 so excited because we ______ 5 there by plane. It ______ 6 a really large plane! In Australia, we ______ 7 a lot of cool things. My dad's best friend lives there. He ______ 8 us the best beaches to go surfing or swimming. I can't surf at all, but I ______ 9 the cool dudes doing tricks. One evening, we ______ 10 a "barbie". We ______ 11 to the beach and ______ 12 fish, shrimp and steaks. It ______ 13 great!

7 Focus on form: Where did you go?

Karam's friend Mia talks to him on the phone about his holiday. Complete the dialogue.

Mia: Hi Karam! You're back from your holiday. Where *did you go* 1 (you, go)?

Karam: I ______ 2 (go) to Australia.

Mia: Wow, Australia! ______ ______ ______ 3 (you, like) it there?

Karam: Yes, I ______ 4 (do). It ______ 5 (be) really fantastic!

Mia: ______ ______ ______ 6 (you, travel) with your dad?

Karam: Yes, it ______ 7 (be) just him and me.

Mia: What ______ ______ ______ 8 (you, do) there?

Karam: We ______ 9 (do) many cool things. Dad's best friend ______ 10 (show) us his favourite places.

Mia: ______ ______ ______ 11 (you, go) surfing?

Karam: No, I ______ 12 (do). You know, I can't surf at all! But we ______ 13 (have) a real Australian "barbie" on the beach, you know, a barbecue.

Mia: I love barbecues! What ______ ______ ______ 14 (you, have)?

Karam: We ______ 15 (have) many yummy things like fish, shrimps and steaks.

Mia: Mhmmm … sounds delicious! I can't wait to see the photos!

Working with words

8 Holiday activities

a) Fill in the missing verbs in the boxes 1–5.

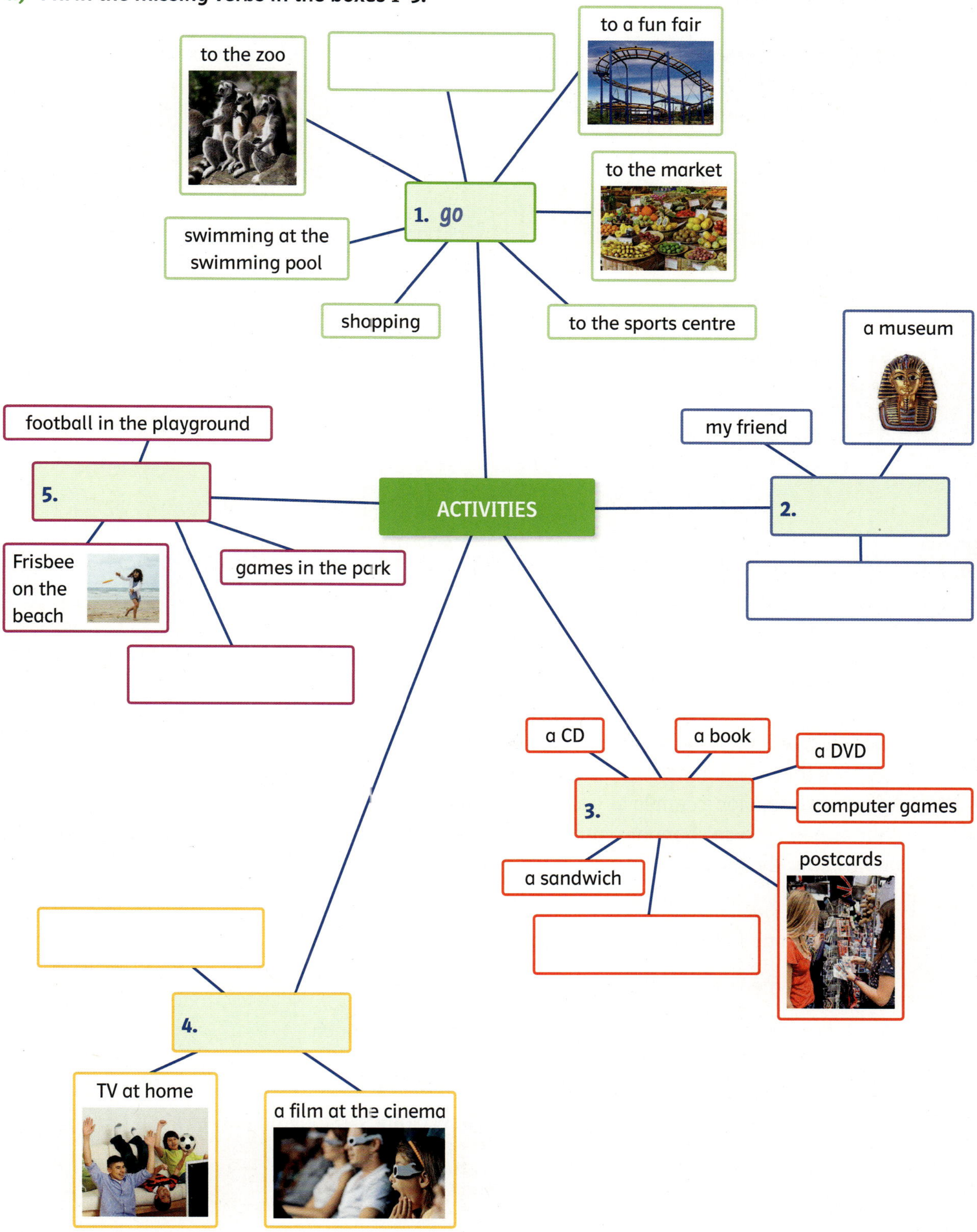

b) Find one more activity for each verb and write it in the mind map above.

Check out

9 Language in use: What are you going to do?

Match the sentence halves.

1. Joshua is going to fly	☐	my grandparents at the weekend.
2. Ruby and Lily are going to stay	1	to Morocco in the summer holidays.
3. I am going to meet	☐	the *Twilight* series in summer.
4. Callum and Mia are going do	☐	at home in July.
5. Millie is going to read	☐	computer games in the holidays.
6. They are going to play	☐	a circus course in the holidays.

☺ 😐 ☹ I can understand sentences about free-time activities.
Ich kann Sätze zum Thema Freizeitaktivitäten verstehen.

10 Reading: Mohammed's holidays

Read the text and then tick ✓ T (= true) or F (= false).

Hi, I'm Mohammed. During the summer holidays my family and I always visit my grandparents in Turkey for one week. My granddad loves going to the beach because he likes swimming. I like swimming too and diving! When we go home for lunch, we always go to the ice-cream shop first and buy a big ice cream. Granny says we should not have ice cream before lunch, but Granddad never listens to her. Sometimes we also go sightseeing, for example to Istanbul. My mum takes lots of photographs when we visit a new place. She also likes to go shopping, and she always buys new T-shirts or caps for my sister and me to take home after the holiday.

	T (true)	F (false)
1. Mohammed and his family always go to Italy in the summer holidays.	☐	✓
2. Mohammed's granddad cannot swim.	☐	☐
3. Mohammed's granddad never has ice cream before lunch.	☐	☐
4. Mohammed's mum likes to take photos in the holidays.	☐	☐
5. Normally, Mohammed and his sister get new clothes in their holidays.	☐	☐

☺ 😐 ☹ I can read and understand texts about holidays.
Ich kann Texte über die Ferien lesen und verstehen.

☺ = I'm very good at this.
😐 = I can do this.
☹ = I need help.

Fact detectives

Unit 16

Activities

1 Reading: Skateboarding safety

a) Read the following text about skateboard safety and underline the words you don't know. Look them up in a dictionary or on the internet.

Safety instructions

Skateboarding can be dangerous. The boards have small wheels and if they hit a stone or a small step, the riders can fall off the board. So it is important to wear the right safety gear.

Especially beginners should wear gloves to protect their hands and also knee pads, elbow pads and wrist guards. Helmets can protect the riders from serious head injuries.

Another problem is other road users. A skateboarder has to look out for people walking along the road, for cars, for bicycles etc. It is not easy to stop quickly and so you have to learn how to slow down and stop when it is necessary. And be careful when you jump off your board: make sure the board stops because it may harm people if it hits them.

b) Match the words with the explanations. Use the text to understand as much as you can.

1.	wheels		You wear them on your hands.
2.	safety gear		Not light.
3.	wrist		It protects your head.
4.	gloves		Things to protect your body.
5.	helmet		To get off quickly.
6.	serious		They are round. Cars, bikes and skateboards have them.
7.	head injury		To be bad for people.
8.	jump off		A part of your body between your hand and your arm.
9.	harm people	7	When you hurt your head.

c) Sort the words from task 1b in alphabetical order.

CB p.130

Keeping fit

2 Reading: How to keep fit

a) **Read through the text and correct the mistakes. Some words must be ~~crossed out~~, others must be filled in. Use a red pencil.**

More and more people exercise to keep fit. Some go running, others like cycling and some go swimming at least once a week. Some have a little computer watch which tells them that they need to do more. When you go for a walk on a Sunday morning, you ~~don't~~ see many people going for a run or cycling.

Doing sports is very good for your body and it helps you to get stronger. People who do sports regularly also do not get much older.

In addition to exercising it is also important that you eat the right things. Junk food, like hamburgers, is really good for you. Be careful with sugar, fat and salt because they are not very healthy if you don't eat too much of them. Sweets for example are really healthy. Make sure you eat some fruit and vegetables every day. And don't forget dairy products. Your body needs them as well. You should also eat carbohydrates like bread or pasta because they give you energy.

b) **Rewrite the wrong sentences and correct the mistakes.**

1. ______________________________

2. ______________________________

3. ______________________________

4. ______________________________

5. ______________________________

3 What to eat

a) **Make two lists with things which you should eat and things which you should stay away from. Use the texts in Units 8 and 10 and the information in this unit (→ coursebook p. 130).**

b) **Find pictures of these things and add them to your list.**

c) **Choose five healthy things and five things you should not eat too often and make a poster.**

Climate and weather

4 Weather quiz

a) Read the questions below and find the correct answers. Write the numbers in the boxes. There are two answers too many.

1. What is a tsunami? C
2. What is a blizzard? ☐
3. What is a hurricane? ☐
4. What is thunder? ☐
5. What is a rainbow? ☐
6. What is hail? ☐
7. What is sleet? ☐

A Little balls of ice falling from the clouds.

B A very strong storm which can destroy houses.

C It is a long, high sea wave. It can be very dangerous.

D A flash of light during a thunderstorm.

E A strong wind with snow.

F A mixture of ice and snow.

G It shows all the colours in the sky.

H The sound you hear when there is lightning.

I A rotating wind.

b) Ask questions for the two new answers.

1. ☐ ______________________________
2. ☐ ______________________________

Animal news

5 What do vets do?

a) Before you read, study the explanations of difficult words and phrases.

1. vet	A vet is a medical doctor for animals.
2. injury	A broken leg is an injury.
3. clue	When you do a crossword puzzle, a clue helps you to find the right word.
4. to smell	A rose smells nice.
5. owner	If you have a pet, you are the owner.
6. medical test	This is a test to check if a person or an animal is alright.
7. to cure	A doctor cures a sick person and then he or she is alright again.
8. medication	This is a drug which you give to an animal or a person to cure them.
9. bones	Bones are the hard structures in your body. They form the skeleton.
10. to operate on	A doctor does an operation on a person to fix a medical problem.
11. to treat	To try to cure a person or an animal.

b) Read the text and underline the words and phrases from task 5a.

Lots of people come to see Mrs Kent with their animals every week. She is a vet, a doctor for sick animals or animals which have injuries.

When you take your pet to a vet like her, the first thing she does is to look at your pet closely and try to find out what the problem is. Animals cannot speak, so the vet has to look for clues like the way in which the animal looks, how it smells or things like that. And of course she talks to the owner of the animal because they know their pets much better than she does. A vet can also do medical tests if necessary.

Then vets have to think about how they can cure the animals. Sometimes they need to give them medication, sometimes they have to fix broken bones, sometimes they have to operate on animals or fix their teeth.

In cities vets treat small animals most of the time, but in the countryside vets also have to deal with larger animals, like horses, and other farm animals like sheep and cows.

But vets also tell you how to look after your pet. So if you have a question about your pet or a problem with an animal, you can ask a vet to help you and to tell you what to do.

6 Do you want to be a vet?

Tick ✓ the right box for you.

I want to be a vet because …

- ☐ I love small animals.
- ☐ I like to help animals.

I don't want to be a vet because …

- ☐ I am afraid of animals.
- ☐ I don't like to touch animals.

7 Focus on function: Asking and giving advice

a) Put the sentences in the correct order and number them.

☐	Carola:	Do you see anything?
1	Carola:	Hello, Mrs Kent.
☐	Carola:	There's something wrong with my dog, and I don't know what it is. Can you tell me what I can do?
☐	Carola:	No, he doesn't. He doesn't touch his food and doesn't drink much.
☐	Carola:	No, not really. He ran around in the garden and when he came back, he went straight to his basket.
☐	Carola:	Rickie doesn't run around as normal. He stays in his basket and sleeps all day.
☐	Carola:	So I shouldn't do anything special?
☐	Carola:	Thanks very much. – You see, Rickie, it's not that bad.
2	Mrs Kent:	Hello, good morning, what can I do for you?
☐	Mrs Kent:	Let me see. He has got red eyes as well. Does he eat and drink as usual?
☐	Mrs Kent:	No, I don't. His tongue looks normal. I don't think it is serious. Do you know what he did yesterday?
☐	Mrs Kent:	No, not for the moment. I think he needs a good rest and then we'll see.
☐	Mrs Kent:	Okay, first tell me a little more about your dog.
☐	Mrs Kent:	Okay, Rickie. Now let me look into your mouth.
☐	Mrs Kent:	Well, perhaps he ate something bad. I think you should take him back to his basket, give him enough to drink and wait one more day. I'm sure he'll get well soon.

4.29 9g54t6

b) Listen and check.

c) Write down sentences in which Carola asks the vet what she should do.

____

____

d) Write down sentences in which the vet tells Carola what she should do.

____

____

Unit 1 Welcome

task 10
6A–9A: TIME **3C–9C:** VILLAGE **1E–4E:** BIKE
4H–8H: WORLD **1K–4K:** CITY **2D–2F:** FIT
8C–8F: GATE **9A–9F:** ELEVEN **10D–10K:** TEENAGER

task 11
1: Hi Dad, this is Rudi. **2:** Hi, Rudi. **3:** Hi, Mr Canelli.
4: What about you? What's your name?
5: My name's Harry. **6:** Harry? Nice name.
7: Thank you, Mr Canelli. **8:** Right, off you go. …

Unit 2 My school is cool

task 10
2: c **3:** a **4:** a **5:** b **6:** c **7:** b

task 11
3: red **4:** in **5:** on **6:** next to **7:** under **8:** desk
9: apple **10:** in

Unit 3 My family and my friends

task 7
2: thirty-four **3:** forty **4:** six **5:** fourteen **6:** three

task 8
Hi, I'm Claire, and what is your name? How old are you? Where do you come from and where do you go to school? Do you have (any) brothers or sisters?

Unit 4 My day

task 7
2: b **3:** c **4:** a **5:** c **6:** b **7:** c **8:** b

task 8
1: When does Howard get up? At half past six. / He gets up at half past six.
2: When does Howard have breakfast? At a quarter past seven. / He has breakfast at a quarter past seven.
3: When does Howard go to school? At half past eight. / He goes to school at half past eight.
4: When does Howard have lunch? At a quarter to twelve. / He has lunch at a quarter to twelve.

Unit 5 Shopping

task 8
2: bottle **3:** else **4:** pounds **5:** I'm sorry **6:** bars
7: Anything **8:** thanks **9:** That's **10:** Here **11:** change

task 9
How much is a ruler? – It's fifty pence. – Thanks very much.
How much is the cheese? – It's £1.89 a pound. – Thanks very much.
How much are the batteries? – They are 99 pence each. – Thanks very much.

Unit 6 Fun with games

task 5
2: dice **3:** houses **4:** land **5:** must
6: at the weekend **7:** lunch **8:** after breakfast
9: the evening **10:** different

task 6
1: "Happy families" is a game for four players. There are 44 picture cards, and the players try to get sets of four cards.
2: First, shuffle the cards.
3: After that, every player gets 11 cards.
4: Now the game can start: The first player asks another player for a card he/she needs.
5: If the answer is yes, the first player gets the card and can continue. If the answer is no, it's the other player's turn.
6: If a player has a complete set of four cards, he/she puts them on the table.
7: The winner is the first player with no cards in his/her hands.

Unit 7 My time – my activities

task 7

1: Marty likes reading books. He's also good at reading fast. **2:** George loves drawing manga cartoons. He is very good at it. **3:** Dan and Hamid like playing football. They're quite good at doing ball tricks. **4:** Charlize loves listening to rock music, and she's good at playing the drums. **5:** Meral and Chris love riding their horses Chipsy and Caesar. **6:** My best friend likes taking photographs of his pets.

task 8

2: F **3:** F **4:** T **5:** F

Unit 8 You and your body

task 8

1: Marietta shouldn't stay up so late. **2:** Olivia should have a healthy breakfast. **3:** Pete should turn down the volume. **4:** Timothy shouldn't talk all the time.

task 9

1: Mary's feet hurt. Her feet hurt because she always plays football without shoes. **2:** Joe's fingers hurt. His fingers hurt because he always plays video games and types on his laptop. **3:** Stephen and Dave's ears hurt. Their ears hurt because they always listen to loud music. **4:** Dario's dad has got a headache. His dad's head hurts because he always stays up late and watches TV. **5:** My mum's and my stomachs hurt. Our stomachs hurt because we always eat a lot of sweets in the evening.

Unit 9 At home

task 11a

2: looks **3:** opens **4:** touches **5:** doesn't bring **6:** doesn't play **7:** doesn't like

task 11b

2: make **3:** hide **4:** don't want **5:** don't like

task 12a

In Pippa's room there is a bed with a cool crocodile **teddybear** on it. She has got a new bathtub **desk** in front of the window with a TV **laptop** and a lamp on her desk. Her schoolbag is under **on** the chair in front of the desk. … On the wall there is a lovely poster with a pony **two ponies** in it. There is no **a** carpet, but **and** it is a friendly and very tidy **but quite untidy / but quite messy** room.

task 12b

Sample text basic and advanced

In Pippa's room there is a bed with a (cute) teddy bear on it. She has got a new (big/nice/…) desk in front of the window with a laptop and a lamp on it. Her schoolbag is on the chair in front of the desk. On the wall there is a lovely poster with two ponies in it. There is a (green) carpet in her room (, too). She has got lots of school things in her room. (There is a school book and a pencil case on the floor). Her room is (looks a bit) messy/untidy. / It isn't a (very) tidy room, but it is friendly.

Unit 10 Food

task 12a

Paula talks about the food she eats for breakfast, lunch and dinner.

task 12b

2: T **3:** T **4:** F **5:** F

task 12b

2: glass **3:** fruit **4:** cafeteria **5:** dish **6:** dessert **7:** dinner

Unit 11 Stormy weather

task 9

1: If it's cloudy, there are many clouds in the sky. **2:** Temperatures in summer can be very high at around 35 °C. **3:** Rain is water that falls from the sky. **4:** There are four seasons; we call them spring, summer, autumn and winter. **5:** A weather forecast says what the weather will be like in the future.

task 10

2: F **3:** T **4:** F **5:** T

Unit 12 Adventure in Grumpland – a play

task 7

2: Kip **3:** Chief Guard **4:** Lucy **5:** Wizard

task 8

2: closed **3:** went **4:** was **5:** stood **6:** opened **7:** couldn't **8:** said **9:** was **10:** didn't **11:** liked **12:** was **13:** took **14:** sat **15:** took **16:** put **17:** couldn't

Unit 13 Birthdays

task 6

2: got **3:** had **4:** posted **5:** called **6:** wanted **7:** celebrated **8:** helped **9:** made **10:** started **11:** gave **12:** texted **13:** sang

task 7

2: I got a new mobile. **3:** Did your grandma make a cake for you? **4:** He didn't have time. **5:** What did you give her as a present?

Unit 14 Animals

task 8

2: Where **3:** What **4:** why **5:** Did **6:** What **7:** What

task 9

2: Two years ago the Webbers visited an animal shelter.
3: You can see lots of exotic animals at the zoo.
4: When my pet rat was sick, I took him to the vet.
5: You should always keep the cage of your budgie clean.

Unit 15 Going on holiday

task 9

1: Joshua is going to fly to Morocco in the summer holidays. **2:** Ruby and Lily are going to stay at home in July. **3:** I am going to meet my grandparents at the weekend. **4:** Callum and Mia are going do a circus course in the holidays. **5:** Millie is going to read the *Twilight* series in summer. **6:** They are going to play computer games in the holidays.

task 10

2: F **3:** F **4:** T **5:** T

Bildquellen

U1 moodboard / Corbis; **4.1** white / Fotolia; **4.2** createur / Fotolia; **4.3** white / Fotolia; **4.4** white / Fotolia; **16** adogslifephoto / Thinkstock; **17** Juanmonino / Thinkstock; **18.1** Jack Hollingsworth-Photodisc / Thinkstock; **18.2** Jack Hollingsworth-Photodisc / Thinkstock; **18.3** Jack Hollingsworth-Photodisc / Thinkstock; **18.4** Jack Hollingsworth-Photodisc / Thinkstock; **18.5** Jack Hollingsworth-Photodisc / Thinkstock; **18.6** alexei_tm / Thinkstock; **26** dionisvero / Thinkstock; **29.1** lindavostrovska / Thinkstock; **29.2** Peter Zijlstra / Thinkstock; **29.3** Alberto Martelli / Thinkstock; **29.4** Christopher Brignell / Thinkstock; **29.5** yamix / Fotolia; **29.6** Mark Herreid / Thinkstock; **29.7** TeodoraDjordjevic / Thinkstock; **29.8** MH Foto-Design; **29.9** Getty Images / Thinkstock; **29.10** MH Foto-Design; **29.11** Getty Images / Thinkstock; **29.12** chengyuzheng / Thinkstock; **29.13** Barbara Pheby / Fotolia; **29.14** Gyrohype / Thinkstock; **29.15** egal / Thinkstock; **29.16** hidesy / Thinkstock; **29.17** Madiz / Thinkstock; **30.1** Getty Images / Thinkstock; **30.2** Dimijana / Shutterstock.com; **30.3** TeodoraDjordjevic / Thinkstock; **31.1** sulupress / Fotolia; **31.2** VRD / Fotolia; **33.1** moodboard RF / Thinkstock; **33.2** Brainsil / iStockphoto.com; **33.3** Mark Bowden / Thinkstock; **33.4** davidpalau / Thinkstock; **33.5** Fuse / Thinkstock; **33.6** dolgachov/ Thinkstock; **35** Ann Worthy / Thinkstock; **37.1** sumnersgraphicsinc / Thinkstock; **37.2** Marina Lohrbach / Fotolia; **37.3** Littlekidmoment / Shutterstock.com; **37.4** Martindh / Thinkstock; **44** Jacek Chabraszewski / Thinkstock; **48** Andy Medina / iStockphoto.com; **53** Martina Draper; **54.1** Barbara Pheby / Fotolia; **54.2** vectormania / Thinkstock; **54.3** Alberto Martelli / Thinkstock; **54.4** Andreas F. / Fotolia; **54.5** Remus Moise / Thinkstock; **55.1** akulamatiau / Fotolia; **55.2** unalozmen / Thinkstock; **55.3** Fotosearch / Ingram Publishing; **55.4** yamix / Fotolia; **55.5** levkr / Thinkstock; **55.6** anna1311 / Thinkstock; **55.7** nixoncreative / Thinkstock; **55.8** liveostockimages / Fotolia; **55.9** Lars Nilsson / Thinkstock; **55.10** fotofermer / Thinkstock; **55.11** Magone / Thinkstock; **55.12** Alberto Martelli / Thinkstock; **56.1** Dizzy / iStockphoto.com; **56.2** MH Foto-Design; **56.3** atoss / Fotolia; **56.4** MH Foto-Design; **56.5** Viktar / Thinkstock; **56.6** MH Foto-Design; **56.7** Janusz Z. Kobylanski / Fotolia; **56.8** Malyshchyts Viktar / Fotolia; **56.9** Andreas Gayer / Fotolia; **56.10** steve-photo / Fotolia; **56.11** MH Foto-Design; **56.12** zach123 / Fotolia; **56.13** Andreas Gayer / Fotolia; **57** Magone / Thinkstock; **60.1** CroMary / Thinkstock; **60.2** Big Cheese Photo RF / Thinkstock; **60.3** hosseinjj / Thinkstock; **60.4** XiXinXing / Thinkstock; **65** niroworld / Fotolia; **69.1** Denira777 / Thinkstock; **69.2** Tuned_In / Thinkstock; **72** nelik / Thinkstock; **78** sanjagrujic / Thinkstock; **80** Sckrepka / Thinkstock; **83.1** Alexandru Nika / Thinkstock; **83.2** omgimages / Thinkstock; **83.3** Alexey Avdeev / Thinkstock; **83.4** BeSilvestre / Thinkstock; **83.5** Monkey Business Images / Thinkstock; **84.1** fredredhat / Fotolia; **84.2** Monkey Business Images / Thinkstock; **84.3** AlinaMD / Thinkstock; **84.4** Didier Kobi / Thinkstock; **84.5** -101PHOTO- / Thinkstock; **84.6** Andreas P / Fotolia; **85.1** gchutka / iStockphoto.com; **85.2** AlinaMD / Thinkstock; **85.3** andreusK / Thinkstock; **85.4** Digital Vision / Thinkstock; **87.1** Robert / Fotolia; **87.2** kldlife / Thinkstock; **87.3** Jürgen Fälchle / Fotolia; **87.4** Colourbox.com; **87.5** ASIFE / Thinkstock; **87.6** Photodisc / Thinkstock; **87.7** Stockbyte / Thinkstock; **87.8** FlairImages / Thinkstock; **88** homydesign / Thinkstock; **89** Denis Radovanovic / Thinkstock; **90** tanda_V / Thinkstock; **91.1** PicturetakerJoseph / Thinkstock; **91.2** Stockbyte / Thinkstock; **91.3** trubavin / Thinkstock; **91.4** BloomsCoffee / Thinkstock; **91.5** MarianVejcik / Thinkstock; **91.6** Nebojsa Markovic / Thinkstock; **91.7** Igor Alecsander / Thinkstock; **91.8** Andrey Semenov / Thinkstock; **91.9** andreusK / Thinkstock; **92** Wavebreakmedia / Thinkstock